Not · A · Tame
LION

Not · A · Tame
LION

*Unveil Narnia through the eyes of
Lucy, Peter, and other characters created by C. S. Lewis*

BRUCE L. EDWARDS

TYNDALE HOUSE PUBLISHERS INC., WHEATON, ILLINOIS

Visit Tyndale's exciting Web site at www.tyndale.com

TYNDALE is a registered trademark of Tyndale House Publishers, Inc.

Tyndale's quill logo is a trademark of Tyndale House Publishers, Inc.

Published in association with the Loyal Arts Literary Agency, www.LoyalArts.com

Designed by Luke Daab

Edited by Linda Schlafer

Library of Congress Cataloging-in-Publication Data

Edwards, Bruce L.
    Not a tame lion : unveil Narnia through the eyes of Lucy, Peter, and other characters created by C. S. Lewis / Bruce L. Edwards.
      p. cm.
    Includes bibliographical references.
    ISBN-13: 978-1-4143-0381-9
    ISBN-10: 1-4143-0381-5
    1. Lewis, C. S. (Clive Staples), 1898-1963. Chronicles of Narnia. 2. Children's stories, English—History and criticism. 3. Christian fiction, English—History and criticism. 4. Fantasy fiction, English—History and criticism. 5. Narnia (Imaginary place) I. Title.
    PR6023.E926C5329 2005
    823'.912—dc22   2005011083

Printed in the United States of America

11 10 09 08 07 06 05
7   6   5   4   3   2   1

TABLE OF CONTENTS

This work is dedicated to my wife,

JOAN CHRISTINE LUNGSTRUM EDWARDS,

the first in our household to read Lewis's Chronicles of Narnia.

Joan knew their depth, wisdom, and greatness long before I noticed them myself.

This book is my "quilt" for you, sweetie.

Thanks, Joan. Thanks, Aslan.

ACKNOWLEDGMENTS

I first offer my hearty gratitude to Matt Jacobson, my literary agent at Loyal Arts, for contacting me in August 2003 to propose a long-range C. S. Lewis project although he had never met me. Your tenacity and enthusiasm are great gifts. Thanks also to my friend Peter Leithart, a true gentleman and scholar, for recommending me to Matt.

Equal thanks are in order to Jon Farrar, Mary Keeley, and the great staff at Tyndale. I appreciate their confidence in this project and their willingness to take it on in a very competitive marketplace for works about Lewis and Narnia. I'm especially thankful to Linda Schlafer and Joan Hutcheson for their stellar editorial work, and to Erin Marshall for her work on the study guide.

My father, Bruce Edwards Sr., always inspires me by his faith and example. So, too, do my children, Matt, Tracey, Mary, Casey, Justin, and Michael. Your creativity and inventiveness make me want to be a better writer. This is my "song" for you.

This manuscript is the product of many direct and indirect influences, prayers, conversations, e-mails, half-remembered dreams, and "news from a country we have never yet visited."[1] Its beginnings lie in early and late readings of the Chronicles and in countless hours in the company of Mr. Lewis's other works. He is my greatest spiritual influence and the reason for my now and forever remaining a Christian.

Most recently, I was able to work at the Kilns, Lewis's former residence in Headington, England, just outside Oxford City Centre. During the summer of 2004, I had the privilege of serving the C. S. Lewis Foundation at the kind invitation of foundation president Stan Mattson in its summer seminar series, always taught at the Kilns. This wonderful event is overseen each year by Kim Gilnett, Seattle Pacific University's "Jack" of all trades, and Kate Simcoe, SoCal's foremost interior designer and hostess extraordinaire. Imagine staying in the very home where the Chronicles were born, where Lewis dreamed of lions and a faun with an umbrella! Just being at the Kilns inspires, provokes, and chastens. The true origin of *Not a Tame Lion* remains, therefore, in Headington, at the end of Lewis Close, by the fireplace in the common room. Stan, Kim, and Kate: *merci beaucoup.*

There I had superb students and colleagues from all over the United States and from Japan at the two week-long sessions. I thank them for their attentive engagement in our discussions and, most of all, for their incisive commentary on all matters pertaining to C. S. Lewis, including Narnia. I hope for a reunion someday soon. That means you, especially, Kyoko!

Finally, there is a great cloud of witnesses whose work and faith have enlivened, challenged, and emboldened me as I have envisioned and finished this project. The list begins with my brothers and sisters at Bowling Green Covenant Church, who have patiently listened to many sermons inspired by Professor Lewis over twenty years. Special thanks are due to Mark Eberle and Bill Larson, my fellow church elders of more than ten years; their constant encouragement and example have enlightened many a dark night. A host of other writers and thinkers (some of whom I haven't met) have in their own way made *Not a Tame Lion* possible. They are not to be blamed for any flaws in this work but can certainly be credited with inspiring its insights. The list could easily be one hundred names long, but I cite just ten. My most sincere and profuse thanks go to Walter Hooper, Jerry Root, Kay Lindskoog, David Downing, Scott Calhoun, Peter Kreeft, Marvin Hinten, Carol Hatcher, Larry Fink, and Alice Cook.

DISCERNING THE SPIRITUAL WORLD OF NARNIA

"He doesn't like being tied down—and of course he has other countries to attend to.
It's quite all right. He'll often drop in. Only you mustn't press him.
He's wild, you know. Not like a tame lion."[1]

MR. BEAVER IN *THE LION, THE WITCH, AND THE WARDROBE*

Here we go—yet another book about C. S. Lewis and about Narnia in particular. Surely this deserves some explanation and, perhaps, even a defense.

Our experience of the Chronicles of Narnia is about to be enjoined and challenged by their incarnation in a new medium: the big-budget feature film. The first of an intended series of movies depicting the exploits of the Pevensie children and others in the land of Narnia is scheduled for release in December 2005. Such a movie will bring new attention—and certainly a new audience, even a new kind of audience—to the Chronicles that no previous, however ambitious, marketing campaign could ever have achieved. For more than half a century, children and adults of all ages have found their way to Narnia almost exclusively through the written word. Previous dramatizations of the Chronicles—whether in audio, animated, or video format—have made less of an impact on readers because these adaptations have usually been verbatim treatments of Lewis's original narratives that echoed the books and sent their listeners or viewers back to the original works. A new generation of readers and moviegoers will now have a much more momentous choice as to how to enter Narnia.

In time, the movies may begin to rival the storytelling art, characterization, imagery, and themes found in the original Chronicles, which were, of course, keenly informed by Lewis's Christian imagination. It is certainly possible that the new meanings and encompassing vision gleaned from watching the movies will complement and enhance those already experienced in Lewis's written works. It is also likely that by their nature the movies will come to overshadow and overwhelm the reading experience of Narnia—as all movies tend to do—and, in blunting or massaging Lewis's essential spiritual vision, to speak more universally but less particularly to their viewers. The literary premises and spiritual principles that most animated Lewis as he depicted them imaginatively within the Narnian landscape could be lost in translation as the stories migrate from text to big screen, with its special effects and surround sound.

We can hope that this will not be the case, and no one will be happier than I should the movies do justice to these beloved tales. In this book, however, I take nothing for granted. Specifically, I wish to orient the willing reader to what we might call Narnia's spiritual geography—to its ultimately Christian themes with their undeniable center in King Aslan, the Great Lion, son of the great Emperor-beyond-the-Sea. Aslan must again be the one to save Narnia, to rescue it from becoming just one more kingdom swept away in the homogenizing flood of popular culture that jettisons its core convictions and compelling charm.

To my mind, the title *Not a Tame Lion* pays supreme homage to Aslan, Lewis's greatest literary creation. "He is not a tame lion," Mr. Beaver says near the end of *The Lion, the Witch, and the Wardrobe*. In chapter 2, I will explore that statement in some depth within the precincts of the Chronicles, but for now, let me reflect on the relevance of the title to this book's contents as a whole. Without Aslan, the Narnia adventures would have little meaning, less value, and certainly no spiritual poignancy or potency.

Plenty of books feature vagabond children who make their entrance into and exit out of strange and dangerous worlds using their ingenuity, creativity, or sheer bravado, learning their lessons and claiming their renown. But Narnia is not a world one simply passes through on the way to somewhere else, storing up experience for the next fantastic journey. Narnia is a spiritual address, a world imbued with ultimate destinies determined by profound personal choices driven by individual allegiances, either to eternal truth or to temporal falsehood.

Narnia is a cosmos, a world with a discernible beginning, middle, and end, whose ordered existence Aslan sings into being. Under Aslan's rule, there are both a natural order and a supernatural or spiritual order. There are the day-to-day deeds, thoughts, and outcomes wrought by each individual, and there is meaning beyond these deeds, thoughts, and outcomes that points to Something Else and to Someone Else. In this, we discover that our lives are not our own but that they rest in Another.

What we do and who we are not only rest in the plane of existence discernible by the five senses but also inhabit an intangible spiritual realm. One day there will be no distinction between the two planes, and what we have called "the spiritual world" of Narnia will be discernible as the real and only Narnia. Now, the day-to-day may seem, in our dreariest moments, to be all there is; and this flawed perception can evolve into fatal behavior, something that neither Aslan nor Lewis is shy about mentioning.

In this, Narnia is both like and unlike our world. In its likeness, it reminds us of truths long forgotten or stilled in our hearts until stirred by vicarious participation in the company of Aslan and his band of followers. In its unlikeness, it forces our encounter with the unknown and the still-to-come steps in our becoming Real Persons, made in the image of our Creator.

We begin to see our world and our place in it, perhaps for the first time, by seeing Narnia as it is. Our world shares with Narnia the themes of creation, catastrophe, treachery, sacrifice, grace, redemption, love, judgment, and consummation. This is because Aslan, who created Narnia, is a figure of

Christ, who created all things (see Colossians 1:16). That being the case, how could Aslan, the Grand Designer, the All-Powerful Lord, the Sovereign of Man and Beast, possibly be a "tame" lion, caged or bound and subject to the will of another? How could the Creator of this world or of Narnia be anything but wild, free, and untethered, beyond the control or the demands of mere creatures? His thunderous roar, his unapproachable majesty, his irresistible force, his mastery of all wisdom and knowledge, the deep and the deeper magic from beyond time keep him unfettered and self-ruling.

And yet, those who've read the stories of Narnia know that this untamed and untamable Lion willingly surrenders his royal title, his freedom, his power, and his very life to save Narnia from the evil treachery of the White Witch and her followers. In taking the place of the traitorous Edmund, Aslan shows himself at his most untamable. He is willing to obey the rules of Narnia that he ordained even if it means his own demise.

We most accurately discern the spiritual world of Narnia in the biography of Aslan. If, as some say, the Narnia tales resemble in genre the New Testament Gospels (themselves an authoritative eyewitness account of the most important exploits and teachings of the incarnate Son of God), perhaps *Not a Tame Lion* can be thought of as a synoptic treatment of Aslan's character and personality as seen in his encounters with the kingdom under his rule. We come to know him first by watching him relate to others and thereby encounter him ourselves.

Having broadly sketched my intentions for this work, allow

me to say a few things about what I do *not* intend for it to be. There are many admirable works about Narnia in print, some of which may be found in the "Suggested Reading" at the end of this book. I have not tried to replicate their design or their content. The list includes works that helpfully paraphrase and provide the "definitive history" behind each Narnia tale; those that trace all the biblical, mythological, and historical allusions found therein; and those that equip families to discuss the Chronicles more or less devotionally. There are also nearly exhaustive encyclopedias, concordances, and glossaries of Narnia to assist readers who seek a level of detail approaching scholarly analysis and exposition.

Though I hope *Not a Tame Lion* shares the merits of such works, I do not intend to treat the Narnia stories comprehensively or chronologically. The chapters that follow are meditations on significant encounters with Aslan, both by native Narnians and by intrepid Sons of Adam and Daughters of Eve who cross over from our world, including you and me. Seen from one angle, Narnia is built upon nothing but such encounters; we anticipate and long for them, hoping against hope that Aslan will appear and break a spell, defeat an insurmountable foe, and set things right. The longing to see Aslan, to fight alongside him, and to rest and remain in his presence are what anchors Lewis's narrative from the first published Narnia tale, *The Lion, the Witch, and the Wardrobe*, to the final one, *The Last Battle*.

In this light, the Chronicles of Narnia offer us a sumptuous literary version of the longing so prominently displayed in Lewis's spiritual autobiography, *Surprised by Joy*. It has always seemed to me that this most revealing of Lewis's works is the best side-by-side commentary on the Chronicles. Without violating Lewis's well-articulated proscriptions against "the personal heresy"—interpreting an author's work exclusively biographically—I believe that readers of the Chronicles can benefit greatly from exploring how *Surprised by Joy* may shape the Narnian landscape. Attention to the surrender to God of Lewis's formidable intellect and imagination on his improbable journey of faith illuminates not only the backstory of Narnia but, most specifically, the character of Aslan. This will orient our meditations in chapter 1.

I am acutely aware of Lewis's dire warnings about the proliferation of secondary sources that may obstruct a reader's experience of the primary work. Sometimes the sheer weight and volume of such helpful guides undermine the embrace of the work itself. The most important duty of every reader, Lewis always said, is to read the work the author wrote, encountering it as much as possible within the time frame and worldview of its original readership.

Still, Lewis reminds us that there is an equal peril in accepting "the first impression that the old text happens to make on a modern sensibility."[2] This may be the greatest obstacle to salutary reading, because untrained eyes or a "bad instrument" can produce the dual errors of creating "phantasmal objects" and of missing real ones.[3] Thus, Lewis suggests that "to consult a map before we set out" may "lead us to many prospects; including some we might never have found by following our noses."[4]

My hope is to create just such an unobtrusive map and thus to discern and retain, perhaps even to reclaim, the spiritual world of Narnia for another generation of readers. That map inevitably points us toward the sometimes subtle, often dramatic, and always dynamic presence of King Aslan. He is the heart and the soul of the Narnian universe that is always just down the hall from us, hidden in a wardrobe, beckoning from a painting, or calling us home in the deepest regions of our beings. May you find him, not only in Narnia, but in this world as well.

CHAPTER 1

INKLINGS OF NEVERLAND:

C. S. Lewis and the Origins of Narnia

When I was ten, I read fairy tales in secret and would have been ashamed if I had been found doing so. Now that I am fifty I read them openly. When I became a man I put away childish things, including the fear of childishness and the desire to be very grown up.[1]

C. S. LEWIS

SUGGESTED READINGS FOR THIS CHAPTER:

The Lion, the Witch, and the Wardrobe: chapter 5
The Silver Chair: chapter 1

Just when we think we have outgrown fairy tales— and the influence they wield over our imaginations—a beloved character or startling image from a childhood story our parents read to us reminds us of a time when we truly cared about something innocent, magical, and true. Being grown up doesn't mean that we've satisfied the longing for these things but only that we have lost our pathway back to them. Perhaps we didn't read fairy tales in our youth but discovered their allure later in life, astounded by the freshness and power of their vision. That vision is inherent not only in this or that story but also in the nature of *faërie* itself, with its power to instill in us the desire for a strange, new, wonder-filled world, an enchanted cosmos or Neverland of our own. This world is not so much a place of retreat or escape as of renewal and rebirth. Can there really be such a place?

C. S. Lewis suggests a reason for this longing—why it exists and how it can be fulfilled. To see this for ourselves and to witness it in Narnia, we should learn more about Lewis's journey to faith, a spiritual quest that illumines the origins of Narnia as well as our own response to Aslan and his kingdom. Let's begin with a quick review of Lewis's life and career and then circle back for a closer look at the childhood and adolescence in which his fascination with fairy tales began.

OUT OF THE SHADOW-LANDS

Lewis died the same day that President John F. Kennedy was shot in Dallas—November 22, 1963, one week short of Lewis's sixty-fifth birthday. He continues to be remembered by the academic world as a distinguished Oxford and Cambridge literary historian, especially noted for inaugurating rather than climaxing his scholarly career with a magnum opus.

This work, *The Allegory of Love* (1936), demonstrated Lewis's formidable critical talent. His scholarship on medieval and renaissance literature set the standards and the terms of debate in these areas of study on both sides of the Atlantic for decades. In numerous publications over the next twenty-five years, Lewis was both prolific and profound in discussing the literary foundations of Western civilization.

Admirable as his academic achievements are, however, it is not Lewis's scholarly work that we primarily celebrate in the twenty-first century. Rather, we admire him as the author of science fiction, myth, and fantasy and as a popular and influential Christian apologist.

That Lewis should be commemorated for his vocation as an orthodox Christian apologist in a time of ostentatious irreligion, postmodern posturing, and New Age mysticism is one of literary history's great ironies.

If we see Lewis only in his youth, we meet a confused and bitter atheist whose mother's death when he was nine robbed him of joy and serenity. If we encounter him as a World War I soldier, we meet a foundering poet who, while crouching in the trenches of France, jots down a poem ridiculing the "ancient hope" of a "just God that cares for earthly pain" as merely a "dream." If we meet him later at Oxford University, we find a self-described "prig" prepared to enter postwar academic society as one more pretentious professor promoting an uninhibited lifestyle. All in all, the Lewis we meet in the 1920s is one of the more unlikely converts among the literati of his time.

In his superb spiritual autobiography, *Surprised by Joy* (1955), Lewis recounts the circumstances that brought him to faith in God. In the manner typical of his writing, there are no Damascus Road melodramas but instead a series of ruminations about crucial books and providential friendships that led him out of unbelief into principled agnosticism, to benign theism, and eventually to robust, orthodox, Trinitarian Christianity.

After he committed his life to Christ in 1931, Lewis embarked on a remarkable dual career. He maintained his scholarly poise and productivity, astonishing colleagues with his erudition and his prolific publication rate while slowly and quietly building a reputation as a modern Aquinas or Newman, a translator and popularizer of Christian doctrine for a skeptical and credulous age. Lewis created *Out of the Silent Planet* (1938), the first book in a science-fiction trilogy of interplanetary romances, to "steal past . . . watchful dragons"

while promulgating his Christian views.[2] He published his first purely apologetic work, *The Problem of Pain*, in 1941.

In this book, Lewis endeavored to reconcile the concept of a good, all-powerful God with the presence of evil and suffering in the universe he had created. It drew the attention of James Welch, head of religious broadcasting for the BBC, who would inadvertently launch Lewis as a religious celebrity. Welch was so impressed with Lewis's compelling arguments and fresh analogies in explaining the essentials of the Christian faith that he persuaded Lewis to do a series of radio broadcasts that would commence in the late summer of 1941.

Lewis made his debut at 7:45 p.m., Wednesday, August 6, 1941. Later in the evening, air-raid sirens would blare all over Britain, preparing citizens for what might be yet another bombing attack by Germany. But that night a most unlikely new radio personality was born, speaking on the topic "Right and Wrong as a Clue to the Meaning of the Universe." With no practical experience in broadcasting or in addressing such a diverse, indiscriminate audience, Lewis was called upon to rally a fearful, war-beset nation to courage and hope.[3]

Lewis was an immediate sensation, and hundreds of letters, pro and con, poured in from all quarters of the United Kingdom. The BBC invited Lewis to extend his original commitment first to eight, then to twelve, and finally to twenty-six broadcasts over a two-year period.

These talks became the foundation for the book eventually published as *Mere Christianity* (1952), the most widely read work of Christian apologetics of the last fifty years. It continues to be credited with countless conversions and recommitments by such disparate people as the former Nixon "hatchet man," Charles Colson, now a respected Christian commentator and prison reformer; Kathleen Norris, the poet and spiritual memoirist; and former Domino's Pizza magnate Tom Monaghan.

Lewis's reputation as a witty, articulate proponent of Christianity continued with *The Screwtape Letters* (1942), purportedly the intercepted correspondence of a senior devil with a junior devil who is fighting "the Enemy" (Christ) over the soul of an unsuspecting believer. *The Great Divorce* (1945) uses the conventions of the medieval dream vision to recount a man's shattering bus ride to hell. *Miracles* (1947) is a defense of God's intervention in human history—the logic, as it were, of the Incarnation. But Lewis's most critically notable and commercially successful creative work emerged in the seven-volume Chronicles of Narnia, published in single volumes between 1950 and 1956.

C. S. Lewis ("Jack" to his friends and family) remains the most widely read Christian writer of the twentieth and twenty-first centuries, his works explored by evangelicals, mainstream Protestants, devout Catholics, and Orthodox believers alike. All of Lewis's works, save a few anthologies of early literary criticism, remain in print as a measure of his continuing influence. To explain this phenomenon is to go against the grain of a recent popular film that purports to tell the true story of Lewis's relationship and marriage to Joy Davidman Gresham. On our way to Narnia, let us take a little time to rehabilitate the dour, reticent Lewis that many have seen depicted in Sir Richard Attenborough's 1993 motion picture, *Shadowlands*.

The man called Oxford's Bonny Fighter is portrayed in this film as inexperienced with women and children, perpetually solemn, and given to excessive brooding about suffering and God's penchant for using pain to rouse a deaf world to action. Such a man would never attract the following the real Lewis had, let alone the attention of as vivacious and intellectually potent a woman as Joy Davidman Gresham. According to the William Nicholson screenplay, Lewis met Joy and his life finally blossomed. He embraced her exuberance and American brusqueness, came out of his shell, suppressed his doubts, inherited a family, and entered into an idyllic though short-lived marriage stopped cold by Joy's death from bone cancer. At the end of *Shadowlands*, Lewis is shown skulking about, grasping for straws of faith, questioning the existence of heaven, and rebuking those who remind him of his former Christian confidence. This is hardly true to life.

As one who has spent the greater part of his professional career studying Lewis's life, works, and times, I

can unequivocally say that the Lewis of *Shadowlands*—
even conceding generous poetic license—never existed.
The C. S. Lewis known to friends, students, colleagues,
publishers, correspondents, and readers was a gregari-
ous, ebullient, even impish sort of fellow who loved
conversation. In his day, he was the most popular lec-
turer in Oxford, and there was standing room only for
his classroom presentations.

Jack loved to meet his friends—Charles Williams,
J. R. R. Tolkien, and Owen Barfield, a group quaintly
self-labeled as "the Inklings"—at a favorite local pub to
read aloud from their works in progress, down a pint or
two along the way, and entertain anyone who strayed
into their domain. Far from being an austere or humor-
less "fundamentalist," Lewis practiced and affirmed a
cheerful, reasoned Christianity, informed by his ency-
clopedic reading of culture and filtered through his
Irish literary upbringing.

The Jack who eventually met Joy in 1952 had behind him two years of intimate correspondence with
her, the knowledge that she was very familiar with his
story and his theology, and a profound respect for her
own creativity and scholarly prowess. There is no question but that Joy's presence in his life sparked Jack's
further literary output, but the personal transformation
he experienced was much more subtle than that depicted in *Shadowlands*.

The relationship more accurately brought a quiet

renewal, not a radical shift in temperament. By all accounts, the couple made a formidable duo as soul mates united by faith, hope, and love. The movie does cover well the cruelty of their relationship's brevity. Joy was diagnosed with cancer, rallied, and then succumbed. Jack took Joy's death hard—as any husband would. He wrestled openly with God, as he admirably and candidly recounted in his memoir, *A Grief Observed* (1963). Lewis explored his loss and returned chastened but emboldened to his faith.

Lewis's friend Owen Barfield shrewdly gets to the source of Lewis's enduring influence when he says, "Somehow what Lewis thought about everything was secretly present in what he said about anything."[4] Lewis's life was, in other words, thoroughly integrated. His presuppositions about life, faith, and reality; his reason; and his imagination were all surrendered to God, and this spiritual coherence manifested itself in all that he wrote and said.

As a witness to the remorselessly sectarian strife of his native Belfast and dismayed by the confusion about Christ and his kingdom both inside and outside the church, Lewis came to care most about what he called "mere Christianity." His wartime BBC broadcasts and subsequent apologetic works were about the irreducible essentials of the faith that have been central to the creeds of the church since the apostles first announced the Good News. Lewis wanted to share a gospel free of denominational idiosyncrasies, untrammeled by the debris of history, and grounded in the identity and mission of Jesus of Nazareth. This "mere Christianity" focuses on what unites Christians, not on what divides them. The Chronicles of Narnia and the character of Aslan are anchored in this core Christian faith.

SURPRISED BY ASLAN

To pick up the trail that leads to Narnia, we should note the unexpected appearance of Lewis's spiritual autobiography soon after the publication of the Chronicles. While completing the last of the tales, perhaps in 1952 or 1953, Lewis began his most unusual and most personally revealing work, *Surprised by Joy*. In writing this story of "a blessed defeat," Lewis says that his specific goals were to answer "requests that I would tell how I passed from Atheism to Christianity" and "to correct one or two false notions that seem to have got about." *Surprised by Joy* actually does much more than this. When read in tandem with the Chronicles, it provides a dramatic commentary on many of the predicaments faced by the human visitors to Narnia. It seems clear that Lewis had been tracing out the elements of his former personal struggles as well as of his difficult journey to faith in depicting the exploits of the Pevensies and others in the land of the untame Lion.

Though he had been a practicing Christian for almost twenty-five years and a vigorous public defender of the faith since the appearance of his first religious work, *The Pilgrim's Regress* (1933), Lewis had never directly recounted anything about his private life or his conversion to Christ. By fictionalizing in Narnia some of the spiritual lessons drawn from his life (including the undeniably autobiographical *The Magician's Nephew*), Lewis found a meaningful, coherent, and satisfying way to tell his own story. Indeed, it seems that after his own encounter with Aslan, Lewis was liberated to tell the very personal story of his conversion that thousands of readers on both sides of the Atlantic longed to hear.

Lewis was reluctant to cover this ground apart from his decades of private correspondence with fellow converts and fans. No doubt he had the conventional modesty of the spiritual autobiographer who downplays the importance of his life while giving glory to God. He was also convinced that no writer's creative work was especially illuminated by psychological inquiry into his or her life. In his role as a critic and historian of literature, Lewis had witnessed too many works passed off as "literary criticism" that were actually imaginary reconstructions of the author's composing process or thought life—poor substitutes for perceptive attention to an author's text.

Lewis believed that this approach robbed literature of its power and meaning by reducing literary criticism to biographical skulduggery. He rejected out of hand the notion that an artist was obliged to lay bare his private life, warts and all, either for celebrity's sake or for its putative insights into his or her literary works. To accomplish the task he set himself, Lewis explains in *Surprised by Joy* that he had to overcome his "distaste for all that is public, all that belongs to the collective."[5]

So why are we apparently violating Lewis's principles of good readership? We are listening to his life, related under conditions Lewis has set, and linking the facts as he reported them to the stories as he told them. We are residing in Narnia under his passport, using the map he has provided. Who would be a better guide than Lewis himself? Lewis similarly chose a fictional George Macdonald to guide his narrator in *The Great Divorce*. Knowing more about the origins of Narnia in Lewis's heart and mind does not rob us of primary experience, but enhances it. We could also reverse the argument and use Narnia to comment usefully on *Surprised by Joy*.

Lewis temporarily opened his life to the world at large only to the extent that it contributed to his articulation of a Christian worldview. He was not submitting it for approval to the self-styled critics of his career who searched for evidence to undermine his Christian apologetics, as some celebrated recent Lewis biographers have done. Lewis recounted nothing that was not directly related to his purpose, but he gives his readers a warning in the preface to *Surprised by Joy*.

The story is, I fear, suffocatingly subjective; the kind of thing I have never written before and shall probably never write again. I have tried so to write the first chapter that those who can't bear such a story will see at once what they are in for and close the book with the least waste of time.[6]

One man's halting "subjectivity" is his reader's delighted entry into the author's heart and soul!

The Shape of My Early Life (the subtitle of *Surprised by Joy*) succinctly communicates the scope of Lewis's autobiography. It deals almost exclusively with his childhood and pre- and post-adolescent search for "joy" and covers events leading up to and surrounding his surrender to Christ at age thirty-one. In *Surprised by Joy*, Lewis identifies himself as no more and no less a sinner than anyone else, but believes it is chiefly his intellectual and imaginative journey that needs charting. The story of his encounter with Christ is not of a grand repentance from fleshly indulgence, but the slow, powerful recovery of childlike wonder at the world and its transcendent mysteries.

Surprised by Joy thus contains only those people and places, ideas and contexts that helped Lewis to explain his conversion—first to himself and secondarily to his readers. Lewis announces the grand climax of his journey to faith in matter-of-fact, understated terms: "Every step I had taken, from the Absolute to 'Spirit' and from 'Spirit' to 'God,' had been a step toward the more concrete, the more imminent. . . . To accept the Incarnation was a further step in the same direction."[7]

Lewis begins this book with a meticulous but sprightly overview of the Lewis household and his early schooling. His household was a particularly bookish one in which the reality he found on the pages of books in his parents' extensive library was as tangible and meaningful to him as anything that transpired outside its doors. Two childhood influences get special mention: E. Nesbit, whose *Five Children and It*, *The Railway Children*, and *The Amulet* considerably influenced Lewis's Narnia, and Beatrix Potter, whose *Squirrel Nutkin* enraptured Lewis with its concept of "autumn," his first profoundly numinous encounter. Later, he depicts himself and his brother, Warnie, as comrades in arms—absolute confidantes who shared their deepest longings and secrets without sibling rivalry within the secure shelter of their parents' Belfast home.

The precocious young Lewis, denied none of the volumes in his father's library, traveled far and wide in history, myth, and story long before he was shuffled off to boarding schools or ever thought of entering the venerable Oxford University. Warnie speaks to the birth of their creative impulses:

> By the standards of a present-day childhood in England, we spent an extraordinary amount of our time

shut up indoors. We would gaze out of our nursery
window at the slanting rain and the grey skies. . . .
But we always had pencils, paper, chalk, and
paintboxes, and this recurring imprisonment gave
us occasion and stimulus to develop the habit of creative imagination. . . . And so, my brother's gifts began to develop: and it may not be fanciful to see, in
that childhood staring out to unattainable hills,
some first beginnings of a vision and viewpoint that
ran through the works of his maturity.[8]

Out of their nighttime conversations and daytime rev-
eries, often inside the literal wardrobe of their Belfast
home, came Boxen, Lewis's fictionalized world of talking animals. As Walter Hooper, Lewis's literary biogra-
pher, tells us, "At about the age of six, C. S. Lewis
invented the imaginary world of 'Animal Land' or
'Boxen,' as it later came to be called, and over the next
few years he wrote numerous stories and histories about
'the dressed animals' which inhabited it. [It] is remarkable that a boy could write so well and could sustain a
single story over a hundred pages."[9]

These stories, clever as they are, betray the extent
to which the enterprising Lewis was striving to please
his father and to find a pathway into the adult world of
his stuffy dinnertime table talk about Belfast politics
and business transactions. Lewis's creatures debate political issues, quarrel over their own importance, and

generally reflect the common and mundane facts of the "real world."

There's no "deeper" or, for that matter, "deep" magic to be observed in Boxen; Narnia is surely glimpsed there to some degree, but through a glass darkly. Lewis was not destined to write realistic novels about contemporary politics; rather, he was born to explore the supernatural and the ineffable in the genre he grew up loving the most: the fairy tale. He was well caught in its grip by the time the illness and death of his mother, Flora, shattered the tranquility and sanctity of the Lewis home when he was only nine. Lewis then recounts the sometimes melancholy but ultimately salutary search for the security and settledness he had taken for granted during the peace and grace of his early childhood. This search ended with the surprise discovery that such security is not the goal of human life and that, in seeking it, one will surely not find it. This theme—the longing for joy and the uncovering of its true source—permeates the rest of *Surprised by Joy* and undergirds the adventures of Narnia.

In the epigraph for this chapter, Lewis mentions reading fairy tales at ten years old "in secret." This would have been within a year of his mother's death, surely the most important event in the lives of widower Albert Lewis and the young Lewis brothers, Warnie and Jack (or "Jacksie," as Lewis renamed himself at age three). Flora's passing set in motion years of doubt, sadness, and alienation between Lewis and his father, and it strained and stained the image of his father in him. Albert Lewis was "all business and bottom line"—no fairy tales for him. Albert's stolid resignation to a bleak and lonely future forced his benighted realism on the household: buck up, be brave, be quiet. The thought of being discovered reading such childish fare as fairy tales in a house filled with weighty books of science, history, and economics terrified the heartbroken Jack, who had only his brother to share his sorrow. Albert lacked the resources for coping with his wife's illness and death, and he did not have the psychological capacity to rear his sons alone. He dispatched them to boarding schools hither and yon as his own grief consumed and debilitated him for most of his remaining life.

The effects on Lewis were dramatic, traumatic, and immediate. Feeling dispossessed and abandoned by his father, he turned more inward to myth and fairy tale as an outlet for creative expression and as a refuge during a tumultuous adolescence. There he found "the scent of a flower we have not found, the echo of a tune we have not heard, news from a country we have never yet visited," a classic statement from his most famous sermon, "The Weight of Glory," of the elusive joy we seek.[10] By "joy," Lewis did not mean momentary pleasure, but the sublime experience of the transcendent, that glimpse of the eternal that is only fleetingly available in earthly loves and in aesthetic experience. Once upon a time, in childhood, he had it, or thought he did.

The retrospective adult Lewis discovers that joy is found only in knowing his Creator and Savior, who invented world and word, person and personality.

In describing his progression toward faith, Lewis paints fascinating pictures of turn-of-the-century Britain, especially of its private-school system and the tribulations of a nonathletic boy whose aesthetic sensibilities were manifestly out of step with those of his peers—painful remembrances first rehearsed in the lives of Eustace and Jill in *The Silver Chair*. In his search for solace, Lewis first embraced what he referred to as "Northernness," the key elements of Norse mythology that embodied "otherness" for him and offered an escape from the mundane realities and stifling conformity of boarding school. Before his return to faith, Lewis would explore the occult, sample Eastern mysticism, and embrace philosophical idealism—all stopping points on his way to accepting the compassionate, incarnate Deity of Christianity.

Lewis depicts his steady ascent of mind and heart—both reason and imagination—toward the renewal of his preadolescent faith as resulting from his propitious encounter with two religious authors and three other key individuals. He cites each of them as a critical catalyst to these gradual but permanent changes in his worldview.

The first of these was George MacDonald, the nineteenth-century Scottish Congregationalist minister and novelist whose *Phantastes* and *Lilith* Lewis first read at age nineteen. These works baptized Lewis's imagination, preparing in him the idea of a preternatural world beyond the strict materialism he had grown so tired of. MacDonald, like Nesbit and Potter, kept alive in Lewis the promise of a Neverland whose enchantments were more appealing than the reality of this world. MacDonald's collected sermons were later essential to Lewis's growing understanding of his faith, and Lewis frequently referred to MacDonald as his mentor.

The popular London journalist and sprightly Christian apologist G. K. Chesterton was the second influential author. *The Everlasting Man*, Chesterton's portrait of Christ and of his impact on culture, offered Lewis his first plausible Christian theory of history. Lewis adopted Chesterton's wit and cunning in diagnosing the ills of his time, and Chesterton's startling use of metaphor and paradox became hallmarks of his own apologetics. Lewis said, "In reading Chesterton, as in reading MacDonald, I did not know what I was letting myself in for. A young man who wishes to remain a sound Atheist cannot be too careful of his reading. . . . God is, if I may say it, very unscrupulous."[11]

Apart from his voluminous reading—and Lewis may reign as the original multiculturalist for the inclusivity of his reading—three persons stand out as particular provocateurs. The first is William Kirkpatrick, whom Lewis called the "Great Knock." Kirkpatrick had been Albert Lewis's tutor, and he was

Lewis's last real teacher before he entered Oxford. Albert finally responded to his son's impassioned plea to rescue him from his most recent dreadful boarding school and dispatched him to Kirkpatrick, then a retired schoolmaster. Kirkpatrick taught Lewis a fierce and exaggerated form of Socratic dialogue, a give-and-take analysis built on the relentless probing of an opponent's position.

Lewis described Kirkpatrick as the man closest to being a "purely logical entity" that he had ever known.[12] Kirkpatrick interrogated his pupil daily to help him master polemics and debate, teaching him to marshal his arguments and to be precise in definition. Under his tutelage, Lewis put on intellectual muscle that complemented his creative faculties. Lewis admired Kirkpatrick and tried all his adult life to think like he did, saying that he was "a man who thought not about you but about what you said. . . . Here was talk," Lewis concluded, "that was really about something."[13] As an atheist, Kirkpatrick did not directly support Lewis's metaphysical yearnings, but he infused him with the idea that while reason alone can never bring an inquirer to ultimate truth, it is the principal foundation for all credible, defensible belief. No doubt the Great Knock's interrogative style inspired the character of Professor Kirke in *The Lion, the Witch, and the Wardrobe*—minus the unbelief, of course.

No less important to Lewis was his boisterous

encounter and subsequent friendship with Owen Barfield, whom he met at Oxford in 1916. Barfield, a keen dialectician and a lawyer by trade, helped to sharpen Lewis's understanding of both reason and faith. In their "Great War," a vibrant correspondence between the two over many years, Lewis and Barfield debated the meaning of the supernatural and the role of God in history. Barfield's greatest contribution to Lewis's journey of faith, however, was in demolishing Lewis's "chronological snobbery," the "uncritical acceptance of the intellectual climate common to our own age and the assumption that whatever has gone out of date is on that account discredited."[14]

Freed from the notions that the past is invariably wrong and that the present is always the barometer of truth, Lewis was able to embrace the possibility that the ancient Christian narrative could be true and valid even in the twentieth century. Impressed by Barfield's commitment to "deep philology" and aware of the cognitive power of metaphor, Lewis described language as incurably "mythopoeic," that is, as mythmaking. Language used to create myth inevitably and simultaneously links hearers/readers to items, persons, and relations on several planes of existence, while also pointing them backward and forward to ever deeper, more resonant layers of meaning that lie beyond any single soul, lifetime, or civilization into eternity.

Barfield set Lewis up for the final blow to his fading

atheism, which would come from another Oxford friend and companion, the devout Catholic and future Middle-Earth architect, J. R. R. Tolkien. One cannot stress too strongly Tolkien's role in overcoming Lewis's objections to the possibility that Christianity could be true. Both Tolkien and Lewis had been steeped in the traditions of ancient Greco-Roman, Celtic, and Norse mythology and the mythical landscapes of Arthurian Britain. When they first met in May 1926, they had much more in common than they could have imagined.[15]

Tolkien and Lewis regarded imagination as an organ of truth—a way of knowing and seeing that complements the role of reason without displacing it. Tolkien led Lewis to the conclusion that while Christianity may comprise a mythology of sorts, it is "the true myth, myth become fact," one in which Lewis could place his full confidence—heart, mind, and soul. Christianity fulfilled (and filled in) the many plots and prophecies hinted at in ancient tales and traditions.[16]

Surprised by Joy is a special gift to Narnia lovers, for in it we learn how indebted Lewis was to a romantic view of history and culture. This is the atmosphere that permeates Narnia, exemplified in such characters as Professor Kirke, Mr. and Mrs. Beaver, Puddleglum, and, of course, Aslan. Reason and imagination are held in tension at all times and neither is allowed to dominate or cancel the other. Lewis explicates in *Surprised by Joy* and dramatizes in Narnia that reason and imagination must each bow to revelation, for only therein lies their redemption and their potential utility in navigating this and other worlds.

In Kirkpatrick and Barfield, Lewis touched on the power of reason and rationality. In MacDonald, Chesterton, and Tolkien, he experienced the power of the imagination. In Christ, Lewis embraced the author of both. There is no more moving or relevant passage in *Surprised by Joy* than that which captures the surrender, both mind and heart, of this "most reluctant convert" to his Lord:

> You must picture me alone in that room in Magdalen, night after night, feeling, whenever my mind lifted even for a second from my work, the steady, unrelenting approach of Him whom I so earnestly desired not to meet. That which I greatly feared had at last come upon me. In the Trinity Term of 1929 I gave in, and admitted that God was God, and knelt and prayed: perhaps, that night, the most . . . reluctant convert in all England. I did not then see what is now the most shining and obvious thing; the Divine humility which will accept a convert even on such terms.[17]

These words might as easily have been spoken by Edmund or Emeth, Jill or Eustace; that Lewis had already captured these lessons in fiction allowed him now to say in straightforward nonfiction prose what he once said in the Chronicles, that "there is no other stream."[18]

RE-ENCHANTMENT AND IMAGINATION

In some ways, it would have been surprising if Lewis had not, like his close friend, Tolkien, authored works of *faërie* lands, for such reading had animated and comforted both of them throughout their lives. As Lewis famously said to Tolkien early in their friendship, "Tollers, people don't write the books we want, so we have to do it for ourselves."[19]

What kind of books did Lewis and Tolkien want? Simply put, they were stories of derring-do—daunting quests populated by fantastic yet credible characters traversing romantic landscapes that intrigue and delight through repeated encounters. Such tales feature a central theme that uplifts our spirits while challenging the accepted wisdom of the present age, pushing us toward the true reality. Lewis and Tolkien coveted books that offered a portal to another world, an authentic Neverland in which justice reigned and the good, the true, and the beautiful were honored and celebrated.

For Lewis and Tolkien—and the other Inklings—imagination was not just the proverbial muse for creating literature or art, but the primary means by which we make sense of the big picture behind the world at large, whether past, present, or future. Reason may give us the facts, but the imagination enables us to put them in meaningful order. Imagination provides the rationale for trusting reason in the first place and helps us to grasp the gestalt of life's meaning—its enchanted core. In the Narnia Chronicles, Lewis imaginatively rewards the child and entreats the adult with the same rigor of re-enchantment found in the fairy tales and myths he was forced to read in secret but now exhorts us to read openly.

Re-enchantment restores an original enchantment, making possible a fresh encounter with the world created by the original spell and un-inhibiting the seeker who desires to embrace the cosmos as it once was and as it might still be, or be again. The "original spell," of course, is our creation in the image of God, who has spoken or "spelled" our world into existence by his mighty Word. The gospel is a "good-spell," a good word that will save us if we believe it.

In reading Narnia, we come to understand imagination as the divinely given human faculty of comprehending reality through images, pictures, shapes, and patterns, seeing what was, what is, and what could be through artistic re-presentation. Imagination is the counterpart and complement to reason. We come to know what is true through words and propositions, and through what is mediated in the heart's "groanings too deep for words" (Romans 8:26, NASB). By the imagination, sculptors and writers, painters and photographers, metalsmiths and quilters—and also, I submit, journalists and lawyers, scientists and farmers, truck drivers and tailors—grasp, negotiate, and understand the world directly before them and the world just beyond them.

We are able to re-present reality through imagination because imagination engages both creation and interaction with the cosmos, not just static gazing. Through the tools of the imagination, art imitates life and life imitates art, and reality seeps through both. The products of creative imagination become part of the reality that is, in turn, engaged by that same imagination. Our encounter with art helps us to defamiliarize what has become habitual and mundane in our world and allows us to re-vise our art (literally to *re-see* it as it is), thus permitting godly change and renewal. Great hymns, novels, movies, and sermons can all do this.

The Christian imagination at work in Narnia and in Tolkien's Middle-Earth is illuminated by revelation, by the life and light of Jesus Christ. It is "seeing with the heart," as the apostle Paul puts it in his prayer for the Ephesians:

> *I pray also that the eyes of your heart may be enlightened in order that you may know the hope to which he has called you, the riches of his glorious inheritance in the saints, and his incomparably great power for us who believe.* EPHESIANS 1:18-19

This is one of Paul's most arresting metaphors. Clearly, "the eyes of [our] heart" must sometimes be further enlightened for us to understand what logic alone cannot reveal. We can be oblivious to things that God wishes us to know but that we cannot apprehend only with our minds. We may read the New Testament and come to know Jesus intellectually as a man with a message, but if we learn to "see with the heart," he becomes more than that. The Son of God is also a Shepherd, the King of kings, the Morning Star, the Way, the Truth, and the Life. He is a Lamb and, most certainly, a Lion. These images are all true, and they are all captured first in the heart and then with the intellect.

NOT A TAME AUTHOR

If one were to explain the theological and aesthetic premises behind C. S. Lewis's construction of the Chronicles of Narnia, they would look something like this:

> The world as we know it is not the world as it once was. The world as we see it and experience it is not the world as it was originally designed and ordained to be. It is now a world of spoiled goodness, of decay. It is withstood and understood only by those with an unfathomably wild anticipation of a soon, sure redemption. The world of shadows, almosts, neither/nors, close calls, and what-ifs will give way to the bright sunshine of a world that is free of evil, pain, and death.
>
> Secret facts inform our every attempt to ex-

plain, or explain away, the universe and our place in its shadow-lands. In all of our millennia on earth, no civilization has been entirely able to disavow the stubborn rumors of a Lost Eden, an Elusive Nirvana, or a Passage to Eternity. In the end, these give the truest estimation of our predicament and of our destiny.

These principles were regarded by Lewis, Tolkien, and the other Inklings as foundational to mythopoeia, or the act of mythmaking. For them, *myth* was not a legendary tale of dubious authority but the grand, overarching narrative that provided a reason to be, and to become, for members of the village, polis, and nation touched by its encompassing themes, images, characters, and plot lines.

Neither antihistorical nor ahistorical, myth evokes awe, wonder, passion, and pursuit. A culture's myth explains a people's origin and destiny, orients them in history, guides them in the present, and points them to a future in which they and their offspring will live. It locates them in the presence of their Creator and Benefactor, Judge and Advocate, and answers the questions of their existence. A true myth has the power to explain where we came from, to shape our identity and purpose, to instill hope, to promote justice, and to sustain order. That is why Lewis can describe the gospel in these terms:

As myth transcends thought, Incarnation transcends myth. The heart of Christianity is a myth
which is also a fact. The old myth of the Dying God,
without ceasing to be myth, comes down from the
heaven of legend and imagination to the earth of
history. *It happens*—at a particular date, in a particular place, followed by definable historical consequences. We pass from a Balder or Osiris, dying
nobody knows when or where, to a historical Person
crucified (it is all in order) *under Pontius Pilate*. By
becoming fact it does not cease to be myth: that is
the miracle. . . . To be truly Christian we must both
assent to the historical fact and also receive the myth
(fact though it has become) with the same imaginative embrace which we accord to all myths. The one
is hardly more necessary than the other. . . . Those
who do not know that this great myth became Fact
when the Virgin conceived are indeed to be pitied.
But Christians also need to be reminded . . . that
what became Fact was a Myth, that it carries with it
into the world of Fact all the properties of a myth.
God is more than a god, not less; Christ is more than
Balder, not less. We must not be ashamed of the
mythical radiance resting on our theology.[20]

The only reliable, all-encompassing world story, and
the one integral to Lewis's craft and motive, is found in
the Judeo-Christian Scriptures. It has provided cultures

from Asia to Africa, from Europe to South and North
America with just such a frame for working out our salvation in the cosmos with fear and trembling. It is the
true history of all peoples of our planet, and the only
trustworthy forecast of our destiny. But the biblical narrative has been crowded out or discarded in civilizations
that have ignored its relevant witness and forgotten its
historical impact. How can recovering postmoderns
take a second or third look at its testimony?

The Inklings' answer was to create fantasies and
new myths that could serve as an alternate history, a
winsome, redemptive, inclusive worldview that would
restore personal dignity and a promising destiny to
those with eyes to see and ears to hear. It is the alterna-
tive to the false history written out of a disenchanted
and dehumanizing naturalism that reduces men,
women, children, and even whole civilizations to instincts, impulses, genetics, and environment. The
dreams and visions of these "cosmic accidents" nonetheless point them to longings that they cannot account for in scientific terms.

Lewis is not a tame writer. It is part of our deep
longing to know that there is a homeland where we
truly belong, an enchanted world that calls to us in the
midst of confusion and doubt, a world that we can see
when the eyes of our hearts are enlightened. That longing has seldom been better expressed than in this passage from Lewis's *Mere Christianity:*

If I find in myself a desire which no experience in this world can satisfy, the most probable explanation is that I was made for another world. If none of my earthly pleasures satisfy it, that does not prove that the universe is a fraud. Probably earthly pleasures were never meant to satisfy it, but only to arouse it, to suggest the real thing. If that is so, I must take care, on the one hand, never to despise, or be unthankful for, these earthly blessings, and on the other, never to mistake them for the something else of which they are only a kind of copy, or echo, or mirage. I must keep alive in myself the desire for my true country, which I shall not find till after death; I must never let it get snowed under or turned aside; I must make it the main object of life to press on to that other country and to help others to do the same.[21]

In his fiction, Lewis was determined to turn hearts toward this true country, to write its history in our hearts by drawing attention to the echoes that already exist in our imagination. In his scholarship, Lewis championed works and authors that embodied the mythological premises he treasured, hoping to reveal the transcendence already present in human endeavor that has been obscured by the relentless cacophony of modern education.

From Middle-Earth to Narnia, from Perelandra to Cair Paravel, and on to Mordor and Malacandra, Lewis and Tolkien call upon each of us to re-enchant the cosmos, to keep alive the promise and animate the search for the world beyond the world. The surprising reality of the fellowship of heaven can be glimpsed in Lewis's Space Trilogy, his Chronicles of Narnia, and Tolkien's Middle-Earth. That is what Lewis is talking about in this early review of Tolkien's *The Hobbit:*

> The publishers claim that *The Hobbit*, though very unlike *Alice*, resembles it in being the work of a professor at play. A more important truth is that both belong to a very small class of books which have nothing in common save that each admits to a world of its own—a world that seems to have been going on long before we stumbled into it but which, once found by the right reader, becomes indispensable to him. To define the world of *The Hobbit* is, of course, impossible because it is new. You cannot anticipate it before you go there, as you cannot forget it once you have gone.[11]

In his later review of *The Lord of the Rings*, Lewis defends his friend's choice of genre, explaining that the fairy tale may be the best medium for directing wayfarers to their true homes:

> But why, some ask, why if you have a serious comment to make on the real life of men, must you do it

by talking about a phantasmagoric never never land of your own? Because, I take it, one of the main things the author wants to say is that the real life of men is that of mythical and heroic quality. One can see the principle at work in his characterization. Much that in a realistic work would be done by "character delineation" is here done simply by making the character an elf, a dwarf, or a hobbit. The imagined beings have their insides on the outside; they are visible souls. And man as a whole, man pitted against the universe, have we seen him at all till we see that he is like a hero in a fairy tale? In the book, Eomer rashly contrasts "the green earth" with "legends," and Aragorn replies that the green earth itself is "a mighty matter of legend."

The value of myth is that it takes all the things we know and restores to them the rich significance which has been hidden by the veil of familiarity. . . . If you are tired of the real landscape, look at it in a mirror. By putting bread, gold, horse, apple, or the very roads into a myth, we do not retreat from reality: we rediscover it.[23]

"The veil of familiarity" is a telling phrase; in the realm of the fantastic, within mythical landscapes, vistas, and perspectives, anything might happen, anything be discovered. A reader is not restricted by the colors, shapes, creatures, languages, and predicaments of the "real world." The author of fantasy can use these and also invent more, intermixing them with the familiar and the real to create a secondary world that encompasses and surpasses both. These alternate histories rescue readers from the veil of familiarity by ushering them into a transcendent realm unreachable by mere reason or coldhearted induction. We do not "retreat from reality," Lewis reminds us. "We rediscover it."

This is certainly the case in Lewis's greatest creations: the landscapes of the Space Trilogy, the foreboding domain of Glome in *Till We Have Faces*, and, of course, the glorious kingdom of Narnia. In our adventures with Aslan, Lewis renews in us a longing for "the scent of a flower we have not found, the echo of a tune we have not heard, news from a country we have never yet visited."[24]

Long before Willy Wonka or Harry Potter appeared, Lewis was re-enchanting a cosmos that had been emptied of significance by twentieth-century thinknocrats, who reduced the universe to numbers and human life to bodily appetites and genetic impulses. With a little help from his friends, Lewis has established an outpost on the edge of darkness, opening the wardrobe door to help us find the object of our longing, the true end of our journey.

CHAPTER 2

ENCOUNTERING ASLAN:

The Danger of Goodness

"Then he isn't safe?" said Lucy.

"Safe?" said Mr. Beaver. "Don't you hear what Mrs. Beaver tells you? Who said anything about safe? 'Course he isn't safe. But he's good. He's the King, I tell you."[1]

THE LION, THE WITCH, AND THE WARDROBE

No one who stands two feet away from a male lion ever wonders if he is safe or not. Of course, he isn't! Between meals, lions seem docile enough—animals don't kill for sport as humans do—but they are not the kind of creature one cozies up to. I have been thrillingly close to lions in the tall grasses of Kenya and Tanzania in an open-air Land Rover—that proximity and those paws, not to mention the roar, warned me not to think I was Rafiki in a certain Disney movie. A lion is majestic and chilling, awe inspiring and fear inducing. Far more people are killed by hippopotamuses than by lions in Africa every year, but offer me the choice of outrunning a hungry hippo or outwitting a pouncing lion and—well, on second thought, give me a good coffee-table book on the Masai Mara Game Park to browse.

Susan Pevensie learns that Aslan is not a man but a lion when he is introduced as their benefactor and protector, and we can forgive her impertinent question, "Is he—quite safe?"[2] Mr. Beaver scoffs, and you almost expect him to say, like Digory Kirke, "What do they teach them at these schools?" But he is not used to little girls—or boys, for that matter—and the children are just getting accustomed to hospitable beavers and parcel-carrying fauns. Susan's hoped-for answer, "Of course he is safe, and gentle as a . . . lamb," is not forthcoming.

A safe lion is a contradiction in terms; lions weren't created to be safe for human companionship, to dwell in zoos, or to obey a circus trainer's whims. A safe lion is no help to anyone, least of all to exiled children in a strange land. The Beavers know that if they are to be protected and Edmund is to be saved, they need an intimidating, roaring lion, not a fainthearted, well-mannered one. This explains Mr. Beaver's exasperated response—"'Course he isn't safe"—when Lucy repeats Susan's question.

That isn't the real surprise, however.

Mr. Beaver says, "But he's good. He's the King, I tell you."

A good lion?

What is a good lion—a lion who is good at being a lion? We can imagine a lion who is not—the cowardly lion from Frank Baum's *The Wizard of Oz*, for instance. But that is not what Mr. Beaver is getting at.

Aslan is not safe, but he is good. How is goodness a counterpoise to not being safe? Isn't *goodness* a synonym for *safety?* Isn't it akin to meekness or something like timidity? Not safe but good? Reverse it, and you get the effect: Good, but not safe. Goodness can't be trusted to leave us alone, untouched and unmoved. Goodness makes demands, putting something or someone at risk. Goodness has a very personal price tag.

THE COST OF GOODNESS
Goodness is fierce and furious, formidable and aggressive, shocking and dangerous. My goodness is, and so is yours.

 40

"'Why do you call me good? . . . No one is good—except God alone,'" Jesus says, interrogating a rich young man who attempted to flatter him with facile spiritual etiquette (Mark 10:17-18). This young man was on his way to being endearingly humbled by the Lord, whose approval he sought. *Good* is a powerful word, *goodness* a powerful virtue, and neither term should be thrown around lightly, because true goodness is an attribute of God alone. We know what goodness is by looking at God the Father and considering his mighty acts. If the rich young man was recognizing the Father in the Son, so be it; but if he was merely complimenting Jesus on his fine messiahship, he needed rebuke, not encouragement. When we call someone good, we are saying something deep, meaningful, and piercing, something dangerous.

If Aslan is not safe but good, we had better take heed. The children do not yet know how awful goodness can be. An encounter with Aslan will not leave them unchanged but will alter their concept of goodness forever. In Narnia, goodness is also terrible, that is, capable of inducing terror, not only in the evildoer who trembles at what is just and right but also in those who feel justified and righteous as they are. The terror arises not only out of physical presence—the mane, the roar, the power—but from the holiness, perfection, and majesty of embodying what is right and just. "In [him] are hidden all the treasures of wisdom and knowledge,"

Paul says of Jesus in Colossians 2:3. When Aslan speaks, grown-ups and children tremble, nations recoil, and evildoers cower.

This is not the quality of goodness that we typically meet today. Our goodness is not terrible, or even terribly interesting. Goodness is seen more often, in fact, as weakness, holier-than-thou hypocrisy, shallow inexperience, or exaggerated moralism; at best, it is naïveté posing as innocence, and innocence has a bad reputation. Few writers, poets, screenwriters, or pundits take up the reckless challenge of depicting goodness. Who needs to see goodness? Goodness isn't good for you; it will just make you judgmental.

Goodness, we think, is platitudinous, predictable, and all too palatable—nothing to sink our teeth into. According to conventional wisdom, goodness is boring and banal, as though goodness were so bountiful and unremarkable that we need not exemplify its power or witness to its presence. Good characters die young, but the villain; the rebel; the despicable, coarse, and deceitful; the plotter and schemer—these live long lives of fascinating desperation.

Notice one recent change in our cultural markers. At one time, television networks featured police shows founded on the intrigue of watching a good detective cleverly decode clues and logically apprehend a perpetrator based on his motives, because bad actions imply faulty character. The bad man slips up, and goodness trumps evil because it is superior, not slippery. Today, by contrast, the rage is "crime scene investigation" in which esoteric minutiae lead investigators to momentous crime reconstructions, often years after the crime was committed. The arrest of the murderer or thief is anti-climactic—less compelling than assembling the evidence that shows how the crime occurred. Who needs Columbo or Father Brown? We don't even need criminals, just crimes. We have forensic scientists and computer simulations. Few shows end with "Arrest that man!" Most conclude inside the lab, with someone saying, "So that's how he did it!"

Evil is easy, or at least relatively so. Lewis said of the ease with which he put himself into the character of the tempter, Screwtape, that he needed to do no research or improvisation. He only had to look into his own wicked and deceitful heart. Evil is the opposite of good or the privation of good; it cannot invent or create. It can only spoil or counterfeit the true, the real, and the good. Remove, reduce, or resist the good and you have all you need to portray badness. What is good is harder to capture realistically and to dramatize without pretense or posture. Goodness is difficult because we do not know goodness the way we know evil. In creating Aslan, Lewis had an edge—he had the New Testament.

As film critic Roger Ebert has said, "Deep movie emotions for me usually come not when the characters are sad, but when they are good."[3] True goodness is a revelation that moves us. We did not know goodness could be so good. Selfless goodness, driven by agape love, disarms us by appealing directly to the heart. It is not phony or flimsy, does not manipulate or call attention to itself, and is not mere surface compliance with abstract principles. Recognizing and identifying with goodness require humility—good characters must be bold and courageous, taking no account of consequential punishment or personal glory. What benefit does Aslan gain by dying in Edmund's place in *The Lion, the Witch, and the Wardrobe?* Only the pleasures of obeying his Father and dispensing the Deeper Magic.

As in the Gospel writers' portrayal of Jesus, Lewis rests Aslan's goodness upon his godliness—his truthful, loving, gracious, merciful, consistent, unerring, and brave service to unworthy and ungrateful others at his own cost. Lewis anchors Aslan's words and actions in the name and character of his Father, the great Emperor-beyond-the-Sea. Aslan thus gives goodness a good name, while revealing badness as the illusory, poisonous, self-damning, empty shell that it is. Well-narrated goodness woos us with mystery, poignancy, winsomeness, and authenticity. Goodness interests us when it is daunting, demanding, and dangerous. Like hope, goodness diminishes despair; like faith, it conquers doubt; like love, it casts out fear.

Aslan is not safe precisely because he is good, and

being good rules out safety as a virtue. Goodness is heroic, daring, and risky. The good Aslan is committed to *shalom*, the total well-being of all who come into his presence, and this makes him dangerous. What the Beavers already know—that Aslan will not tread lightly— the Pevensies must experience, and the White Witch will refuse to learn. Such goodness penetrates, leaving us wounded and shaken because it reveals us to ourselves. It teaches us the degree to which we must deny ourselves if we are to embody the goodness of our Creator, who knows better than we do what is good for us.

MEETING ASLAN IN *THE LION, THE WITCH, AND THE WARDROBE*

The Narnia tales, of course, did not begin as moralistic tales fraught with weighty didactic baggage, nor were they targeted for someone's unsuspecting training in discipleship. They didn't even begin as stories at all— they began as pictures. All seven Narnia books, Lewis tells us, began as pictures seen in his head.

> At first they were not a story, just pictures. . . . All began with a picture of a Faun carrying an umbrella and parcels in a snowy wood. This picture had been in my mind since I was about sixteen. . . . At first I had very little idea how the story would go. But then suddenly Aslan came bounding into it. I think I had been having a good many dreams of lions about that

time. Apart from that, I don't know where the Lion came from or why He came. But once He was there he pulled the whole story together, and soon He pulled the other six Narnia stories in after Him.[4]

In pictures and dreams, the adolescent Lewis met the adult Lewis on an even plain. He had carried an image of a faun in his heart for thirty-four years, and finally Mr. Tumnus emerged when Aslan created him in the Narnia of Lewis's imagination.

Narnia is a wondrously diverse land of clever, talking animals, faithful and faithless dwarfs, wicked witches, swashbuckling mice, and Marsh-wiggles—but the most important fact about this world is that it is ruled by the magnificent and glorious lion, King Aslan. Aslan's gentle and fair, but ferociously firm, manner evokes awe, creates joy, and confounds evildoers. He delights his subjects, and all who would live peaceably in his realm, as he reigns under a "weight of glory." Aslan's existence does not emerge from his perfect fit with a preconceived outline of characterization, plot, or theme but from his unwillingness to leave Lewis alone. Aslan is irresistible—or so Lewis and millions of readers have found him.

The name Aslan evokes both anticipation and trepidation. Lewis explains its exotic origins in a letter he wrote to one of his young correspondents after the publication of *The Lion, the Witch, and the Wardrobe:*

 46

Dear [Carol],

It is a pleasure to answer your question. I found the name in the notes to Lane's *Arabian Nights:* it is . . . Turkish for Lion. . . . And of course I meant the Lion of Judah.[5]

Lewis had been working with a Middle-Eastern student who shared Lewis's love for *The Arabian Nights.* In researching the various versions of this famous text, Lewis happened upon Aslan, which he pronounced "Ass-lan." It is charming and endearing to learn the derivation of Lewis's name for his Lion King. It speaks of his continuing interest in the world's stories, his willingness to go beyond typical Western contexts to ground his narratives in the strange and the unexpected, and his desire to invest his tales with an otherness that creates intrigue and mystery. It also indicates Lewis's profound literalism about titles and names, unlike Tolkien's obsessively elaborate naming conventions and intricate map building in Middle-Earth. To Lewis, it made perfect sense to call the Lion by a name that means "lion." A Creator calls things into being, and naming them is a prerogative that he can delegate to his righthand men and women. When God placed Adam in the Garden, God immediately gave Adam the job of naming the other creatures he had made.

When the Pevensie children first hear Aslan's name,

they have an intuitive sense of what it means when Mr. Beaver says that Aslan is on the move:

> Each one of the children felt something jump inside. . . . Edmund felt . . . horror. . . . Peter felt suddenly brave. . . . Susan felt as if some delicious smell . . . had just floated by. . . . And Lucy got the feeling you have when you wake up in the morning and realize that it is the beginning of the holidays or the beginning of summer.[6]

Later, after dinner, they all want to know more about Aslan—all but Edmund, of course—and immediately think of "the first signs of spring, like good news."[7] When they reflect on the fact that he is a lion, they also experience dread and fear. What was *our* first meeting with Aslan like?

For the vast majority of readers, Aslan is happily first met in *The Lion, the Witch, and the Wardrobe*. Within the last decade, the Chronicles' publishers have reordered the Narnia series, placing *The Magician's Nephew* first in the belief that contemporary readers should encounter the seven novels in chronological order according to Narnian time. I strongly suggest that readers new to Narnia should read them in the order in which Lewis published them, beginning with *The Lion, the Witch, and the Wardrobe* (1950). Lewis, however, can be quoted on both sides of this issue, and he was oblivious to many details of his own composing process: "I'm not even sure that all the others were written in the same order in which they were published. I never keep notes of that sort of thing and never remember dates."[8]

I believe it makes more literary sense to begin with *The Lion, the Witch, and the Wardrobe* because of its central image of Aslan as the incarnate Savior and Protector, rather than the Creator. This is where Lewis first met this dangerously good but unsafe Lion in his dreams. There is something magical about slowly and indirectly overhearing things about Aslan, having the suspense build up until (at last!) we meet him.

> But as for Aslan himself, the Beavers and the children didn't know what to do or say when they saw him. People who have not been in Narnia sometimes think that a thing cannot be good and terrible at the same time. If the children had ever thought so, they were cured of it now. For when they tried to look at Aslan's face they just caught a glimpse of the golden mane and the great, royal, solemn, overwhelming eyes; and then they found they couldn't look at him and went all trembly.[9]

Aslan, his majesty unfurled and his authority established, commands his new battalion, augmented by three comrades from the other side of the Wardrobe. Yes, this is the ideal way to meet Aslan—as Lewis did and as Peter,

Susan, and Lucy do. He is good and terrible, with his flash of golden mane, his deep and penetrating eyes. His name, his mane, and his manner command awe, reverence, and obedience. We see him in a close and personal way.

Aslan knows the creatures who are his—he calls them, names them Kings and Queens, bestows upon them their solemn duties, and equips them for his service.

> When the girls had gone, Aslan laid his paw—and though it was velveted it was very heavy—on Peter's shoulder and said, "Come, Son of Adam, and I will show you a far-off sight of the castle where you are to be King. . . .
>
> "That, O Man, . . . is Cair Paravel of the four thrones, in one of which you must sit as King. I show it to you because you are the first-born and you will be High King over all the rest."[10]

Aslan's commission is irrevocable and his commitment everlasting; even when we learn at the end of *Prince Caspian* that this will be Peter's last journey to Narnia, he sadly but heroically accepts this as the will of Aslan. The implication is that, his apprenticeship in Narnia now over, he is prepared for a permanent return to the land of humans where he will continue to serve the Lion of Judah.

THE SINGING CREATOR IN
THE MAGICIAN'S NEPHEW

By contrast with *The Lion, the Witch, and the Wardrobe* with its close-up portrait of Aslan, *The Magician's Nephew*, written last by Lewis (and clearly composed with the advantage of hindsight), emphasizes Aslan's glorious transcendence—his awesome power and authority to invent, create, and foster. This produces its own magnificent first encounter with the Lion, but this time as Initiator and Artist. In this tale, we meet Aslan first as a Singer with a sonorous voice:

> In the darkness something was happening at last. A voice had begun to sing. It was very far away and Digory found it hard to decide from what direction it was coming. Sometimes it seemed to come from all directions at once. Sometimes he almost thought it was coming out of the earth beneath them. Its lower notes were deep enough to be the voice of the earth herself. There were no words. There was hardly even a tune. But it was, beyond comparison, the most beautiful noise he had ever heard. It was so beautiful he could hardly bear it.[11]

In *The Magician's Nephew* we meet Aslan through his song. This numinous moment reverently bypasses the intellect and plays instead on our heartstrings: It is the beautiful noise that is too much to bear. Lewis lets us

experience what the moment of creation sounded like—
not as a "big bang" but as the sweet and melodic voice of
the Son, singing worlds into existence. Digory and Polly
witness the glorious birth of Narnia, still pitched on
the edge of Nothing: "Narnia, Narnia, Narnia, awake.
Love. Think. Speak. Be walking trees. Be talking beasts.
Be divine waters."[12]

In "the deepest, wildest voice they had ever heard,"
with Aslan now singing, now narrating Narnia into existence, the children felt every drop of blood tingling in
their bodies.[13] Lewis complements the reader's visual
images with aural ones that capture a different dimen-
sion of Aslan's power and tenderness, not only in Narnia's creation, but in ours as well. The order is *awake,
love, think, speak.* "Remember your fairy tales," Lewis
says in *The Weight of Glory:*

> Spells are used for breaking enchantments as well as
> for inducing them. And you and I have need of the
> strongest spell that can be found to wake us from the
> evil enchantment of worldliness which has been laid
> upon us for nearly a hundred years. Almost our
> whole education has been directed to silencing this
> shy, persistent, inner voice: almost all our modern
> philosophies have been devised to convince us that
> the good of man is to be found on this earth.[14]

In Narnia, we awaken from our long sleep. The spell
that has darkened our hearts and shackled our souls is

broken, and we can see the world—ours and Narnia's—as it truly is, the creation of a sovereign Lord whose love impels him to create, nurture, and covenant with us. Aslan's creation of Narnia compels us to contemplate our common creaturehood, to fully recognize our finiteness in the context of his infinite glory and matchless wisdom.

Our "shy, persistent, inner voice" is liberated to join the chorus of thousands rejoicing over the creation of Narnia; awake, we also may sing with Aslan, enveloped in the song of the Lion and the Lamb. It is a love song because Aslan is love—and the first command after "awake" is thus to love—to love him and his creatures who are precious in his sight because he has sung each one into existence. From love we are called upon to think, to contemplate his grandeur and his grace and to meditate on our participation with him in the fresh, unblemished world. And thus, to speak, to report what we have witnessed and to express thanksgiving and glory to him who has entrusted us with the care of the world that we inhabit under his dominion.

The Aslan we meet in *The Magician's Nephew* is more cosmic and rules more worlds than we may have realized; his Father is not only Emperor-beyond-the-Sea, but the Father of all life. Aslan is the Lord of the worlds we know and of many that we don't know—he is not a tame Lion and we know he doesn't like being tied down; he has many countries to oversee. He can create out of nothing, make creatures in his own image, and invest himself personally on their behalf. He can lay down his life for them and take it up again, as he has done on either side of the Wood between the Worlds.

This phrase denoting the wooded area between London and Charn or Narnia is taken from the title of a fantasy novel, *The Wood Beyond the World*, by the nineteenth-century novelist William Morris, a writer Lewis loved. Lewis once remarked that there are books whose titles are as satisfying as the stories themselves for the wonder and emotion they evoke. Lewis paid tribute to Morris by using his title as the inspiration for the Wood between the Worlds, a portal through which the progeny of Adam and Eve enter Narnia—much as Lewis uses the wardrobe in *The Lion, the Witch, and the Wardrobe* or the painting in *The Voyage of the "Dawn Treader"* through which Lucy, Edmund, and Eustace enter Narnia.

The Magician's Nephew, set more than half a century before Lucy's discovery of the wardrobe that gives the Pevensie children access into Narnia, is seemingly the first visit of human beings to Aslan's world. It is full of surprises. Among them is the revelation that its young protagonist, Digory Kirke, and his adventurous companion, Polly, are only two of several humans who have been to Narnia. We discover the origins of Narnia and the wardrobe in this tale and find out why the wardrobe is such a magical portal. A third delightful discovery is that the impetuous Digory is destined to become the wise Professor Kirke who laments that his young house guests in *The Lion, the Witch, and the Wardrobe* are not logical enough to understand that "there could be other worlds—all over the place, just around the corner" just as he had experienced.[15] These are all grand secrets that are more fun to learn after we have met Aslan and Professor Kirke than if we had known them from the beginning.

In *The Magician's Nephew*, we witness the end of Charn, a world that has been ruined by Queen Jadis's treachery and her bloodthirsty bid for power. Close on the heels of this destruction comes the birth of a free and sinless world filled with talking animals and breathtakingly beautiful landscapes. The story of Narnia's creation provides a bridge to *The Last Battle* in which Old Narnia gives way to New Narnia, wherein all worlds consist. In each, it is abundantly clear that Aslan, all-wise and all-powerful King of Narnia, can weave wicked and foolish deeds into a pattern of blessing and consolation. Digory did not intend to release evil into the world, but his careless showing off to spite Polly led to this terrible result. Seemingly innocent actions can have powerful consequences, but Aslan is able to redeem both the deed and Digory through his loving, creative care.

Here, as elsewhere in Narnia, mere magic is trumped by true faith and right behavior. Uncle Andrew's quest, like that of Jadis, is to find the right incantation, spell, or amulet that will give him ultimate control of his environment. Both learn that there is a greater power at work in the universe, and the schemes of both are thwarted.

The apple that Aslan allows Digory to take home to heal his mother is perhaps the clearest symbol in the Chronicles. It represents the gifts of knowledge, health, and true life. The same apple that gives life when offered by Aslan brings bondage to Jadis's shriveled soul when she eats of it. The parallel to the Genesis story is evident: first Eve and then Adam were tempted by the serpent to eat from the tree of the knowledge of good and evil so that they would "be like God" (Genesis 3:5). Lewis's commentary on our origins in *Mere Christianity* wisely reflects the central theme of *The Magician's Nephew:*

> What Satan put into the heads of our remote ancestors was the idea that they could "be like gods"—could set up on their own as if they had created themselves—be their own masters—invent some sort of happiness for themselves outside God, apart from God. And out of that hopeless attempt has come nearly all that we call human history—money, poverty, ambition, war, prostitution, classes, empires, slavery—the long terrible story of man trying to find something other than God which will make him happy.[16]

This sordid list of abortive human attempts to find fulfillment, lasting happiness, and peace apart from God parallels the awful state of Charn, whose wicked Queen Jadis caused its destruction, and who now wishes to spread her evil to the human world. Just as *The Magician's Nephew* parallels the biblical story of Genesis, *The Last Battle* (the seventh and last Chronicle) shares much with the New Testament book of Revelation, which foretells the end of our world.

Part of the inside story of Narnia's origins is also tied to Lewis's composing chronology. *The Magician's Nephew* was actually the last of the Narnia Chronicles to be written, though it was published before *The Last Battle*. Placed side by side, the last two novels complete the chronology of Narnia; thus, it is interesting to note that about the time that he was drafting *The Magician's Nephew*, *The Last Battle*, and *Surprised by Joy*, Lewis was also writing about the theological question of eschatology, the study of "last things," as exemplified in his poignant essay "The World's Last Night."[17] In reflecting on how worlds begin and end, Lewis found the fairy tale to be the best fictional vehicle for exploring his theological musings.

CHAPTER 3

VALOR FINDS VALIDATION:
Reigning with Aslan

"But who is Aslan? Do you know him?" [asked Eustace.]

"Well—he knows me," said Edmund. "He is the great Lion, the son of the Emperor over Sea, who saved me and saved Narnia."[1]

THE VOYAGE OF THE "DAWN TREADER"

SUGGESTED READINGS FOR THIS CHAPTER:

The Lion, the Witch, and the Wardrobe: chapters 4, 5
Prince Caspian: chapters 4, 7
The Voyage of the "Dawn Treader": chapter 7
The Silver Chair: chapters 1, 2, 10, 12
The Magician's Nephew: chapters 1, 2, 4, 5, 9, 13, 14, 15

Valor is supreme courage, the boldness to act fearlessly in the face of opposition, the willingness to stand up for truth against all odds—alone, if necessary. Valor measures physical prowess and endurance, as well as intellectual and moral strength. Valor requires imagination, fortitude, and a sound conscience; its power resides in a resolute character invested in virtue.

Valor is tested in crisis and refined in battle; it is steady in defeat or victory. Valor is necessarily public—there is no such thing as a strictly private virtue. What could it mean to be courageous in the dark—to step forward and be counted when there is no one around to count? Cowards lurk in the shadows, relying on anonymity to keep them safe when the tough decisions are made or the tough battles are fought. Allegiances that demand selflessness are forged without the coward's consent or participation. For the truly valorous, their virtue is consistent, whether anyone is watching or not. It operates behind closed doors and in the light of day.

We see valor in Narnia wherever Aslan romps and reigns, wherever his word is revered. It takes valor even to visit Narnia. The sojourner with the vision to understand Narnia's foundations will take pleasure in Aslan's ethics, and in them find validation. His character defines the valor that is characteristic of all who embrace him as their King and Savior. The Chronicles of Narnia include stories of both valor and cowardice.

WHAT DO THEY TEACH THESE CHILDREN? THE PEVENSIES IN *THE LION, THE WITCH, AND THE WARDROBE*

The children who travel to Narnia do not arrive with a lifetime supply of valor. Peter, Susan, Edmund, and Lucy arrive under duress. By their parents' decree, they are fleeing the war and the peril of bombs falling on their city. Their lessons begin almost immediately at Professor Kirke's country home, where they are sheltered from danger and instructed in valor, logic, and imagination. Their journey has an autobiographical basis, as Jack and Warren Lewis received children into their home during the war. What great conversations must have ensued! The story also resonates with *The Railway Children*, an early twentieth-century children's story written by E. Nesbit, one of Lewis's favorite writers.

Thinking they have arrived at the Professor's home for safety and comfort, the children are not aware that they have also been called there to journey into Narnia for a higher purpose—to become Aslan's allies and partners in liberating Narnia and restoring its true royal leaders—themselves. In Narnia, they will learn what it means to be brave, serious, and poised. They will gain the experience needed for becoming valorous leaders by following Aslan's example.

Edmund's betrayal of his siblings and his eventual redemption are also at the heart of *The Lion, the Witch, and the Wardrobe*. Aslan knows before Edmund does that his alienation from his siblings makes him susceptible to the White Witch's cunning. He has come to the Professor's house with a surly attitude, which has bred habits of exaggeration and lying. While the others are content to explore and marvel, Edmund is constantly plotting. In her brief visit with Mr. Tumnus, Lucy has her heart torn by the active oppression in Narnia that turns one Narnian against another, while Edmund's heart is simply cold and ambitious—Turkish Delight will satisfy his lowly aspirations for glory and attention. Lucy's compassion and courage are thus set against Edmund's treachery and dishonor throughout the story until the final scenes unfold.

A key confrontation early in this tale exemplifies the clear thinking and moral courage necessary to ally oneself with the truth and stand by one's testimony. Lewis juxtaposes Professor Kirke's wisdom with the plaintive accusations of Peter and Susan, who fear that Lucy has lost her mind. Her claim that she has been to Narnia marks her in their view as unstable and perhaps desperately ill. Edmund, who has also been to Narnia, conceals the truth of his visit and suggests that Lucy is not to be trusted. The Professor, dismayed that the schools don't teach logic anymore, exclaims, "There are only three possibilities. Either your sister is telling lies, or she is mad, or she is telling the truth. You know she doesn't tell lies and it is obvious that she is not mad. For the moment then, and unless any further evidence turns up, we must assume that she is telling the truth."[2]

In his fiction, literary essays, and apologetic works, Lewis was fond of framing such "trichotomies" that force a choice among three mutually exclusive possibilities upon the reader. He knew that moderns had trouble believing that there could be one single answer, one right way, and the trilemma was a useful way to dramatize this. There is a famous parallel to this scene from *The Lion, the Witch, and the Wardrobe* in *Mere Christianity* that focuses on the identity of Jesus Christ:

> I am trying here to prevent anyone saying the really foolish thing that people often say about Him: "I'm ready to accept Jesus as a great moral teacher, but I don't accept His claim to be God." That is the one thing we must not say. A man who was merely a man and said the sort of things Jesus said would not be a great moral teacher. He would either be a lunatic—on a level with the man who says he is a poached egg—or else he would be the Devil of Hell. You must make your choice. Either this man was, and is, the Son of God: or else a madman or something worse. You can shut Him up for a fool, you can spit at Him and kill Him as a demon; or you can fall at His feet and call Him Lord and God. But let us not come with any patronizing nonsense about His be-

ing a great human teacher. He has not left that open to us. He did not intend to.[3]

This is Lewis's "liar, lunatic, or Lord" construction. It imitates a passage in Saint Augustine's early fifth-century defense of Christianity, *The City of God*, wherein Augustine offers a triad of options to explain the triumph of Christian faith in a pagan culture. At Professor Kirke's home, its purpose is to sharpen and personalize the distinctions among the three options. A trilemma does not offer a simplistic "either-or" but forces a "must be" that requires valorous action and not just speculation. Instead of juggling the possibilities in the air while perpetually postponing decisions, Professor Kirke compels the older siblings to ask themselves who is really credible—the person of faith or the person of skepticism? A larger question than Lucy's sanity is at stake: Is there a world beyond this one, and if so, how does it impinge on our own?

Peter is incredulous at the available choices, but he understands their implications. He blurts out, "But do you really mean, Sir, . . . that there could be other worlds—all over the place, just round the corner—like that?"

The Professor's reply is telling: "Nothing is more probable."[4]

Lewis uses the alter ego of Professor Kirke to foreshadow the disposition required in preparing oneself for a journey to Narnia. One must keep one's wits even in a coat closet; anything is possible! Such openness to wonder is a necessary component for thriving in Aslan's kingdom. When the rumors begin that Aslan is on the move, true Narnians are exhilarated, whereas faithless ones are alarmed.

When Lucy encounters Edmund on his way back from his first encounter with the White Witch, she is animated in her denunciation of the Witch's cruelty, but Edmund simply deadpans, "You can't always believe what fauns say."[5]

Later, with the Beavers, as the other children enthusiastically discuss the time when Aslan will "settle the White Queen," Edmund demurs, "She won't turn him into stone too?"

Mr. Beaver guffaws at such foolishness. "Lord love you, Son of Adam, what a simple thing to say!"[6] But cowardice breeds contempt for the holy and the true, as Edmund, on the make for more Turkish Delight, slinks away to inform his accomplice in treachery of their whereabouts.

The White Witch, with her pretensions of authority and grandeur, is proof of the maxim "a little knowledge is a dangerous thing" because she believes she has trumped Aslan by evoking "the Deep Magic from the dawn of time" to justify her execution of Edmund, a Son of Adam.[7] Unfortunately for her, but gloriously for Edmund, she does not have the full story. She concludes that Aslan is beaten at his own game because the justice demanded by the Deep Magic for the treachery of a traitor is the traitor's death. But when Aslan substitutes himself for Edmund on the Stone Table, he embodies a *deeper* magic from *before* the dawn of time: "When a willing victim who had committed no treachery was killed in a traitor's stead, the Table would crack and Death itself would start working backwards."[8] The Sons of Adam and Daughters of Eve rise to the occasion, valorous in word and deed under Aslan's command, including Edmund, who is seriously wounded when he breaks the Witch's wand, thus ending her rule.

The story could, of course, end there, with Edmund forever crippled by his duplicity and poor judgment, unable to survive, let alone function in Narnia. But this is Aslan's domain and Aslan's story. Edmund is healed by Lucy's potion, forgiven by all those he has betrayed, and restored by Aslan to his rightful reign as one of the kings of Narnia. "Once a king or queen in Narnia, always a king or queen. Bear it well, Sons of Adam! Bear it well, Daughters of Eve!" Aslan tells them.[9]

The significance of this second chance is not lost on Edmund, who becomes a mentor to Prince Caspian and his recalcitrant cousin, Eustace Scrubb. In the epigraph to this chapter, Edmund reflects upon his rescue by Aslan as he responds thoughtfully to Eustace's question, "Do you know Aslan?"

His reply is telling: "Well, he knows me." To know as we are known is the great promise of heaven, and of dwelling in Narnia. Once upon a time, Edmund did not know the cost paid by the Lion for his life. Now he does. The most important, most wonderful thing was not what Edmund knew, but what Aslan did.

"[He] saved me, and he saved Narnia," Edmund confesses. Redeemed and rectified, Edmund is now in a position to train others in the grace and mercy of Aslan.[10]

THE BOY WHO WOULD BE KING:
PRINCE CASPIAN IN *PRINCE CASPIAN*

Mentoring in valor and righteousness is also the thematic center of *Prince Caspian*, subtitled *The Return to Narnia*. On this second excursion to Narnia, will the place we think we knew well have changed, or will it remain just as we left it? What will be our landmarks and anchors if the Narnia we know is not the Narnia we now encounter?

We are told that Lewis originally hoped to call it "Night Under Narnia,"[11] and one can see why: While only a year of earthly time has passed for the Pevensies since their last visit to their kingdom, in their absence, Narnia has aged a thousand years; the memories of High Kings and Queens, and Aslan himself, have faded, and the native Narnians once again find themselves in need of redemption and a rightful ruler to be restored to the throne. Narnian society, set right by Aslan's earlier sacrifice and resurrection, seems to have developed a cultural and historical amnesia, and a dark age has set in. How could this be? What has gone wrong? Narnia's development has been arrested, and painful and debilitating questions have arisen. What should one believe? Why should anyone believe in the old stories? Does Aslan even exist?

For Caspian, the future king, these are not mundane matters. When we first meet him, he is a callow youth in search of his true identity—he must avenge his father's death and rise to the kingly role to which he is destined. Like many young kings in the Bible (and in other world cultural narratives), he is in some ways wise beyond his years, and his greatest trait is his humility. To find and embrace his true heritage, he must hold fast the truths that his loyal counselor and guide, Dr. Cornelius, has preserved and faithfully relayed to him.

"Listen," said the Doctor. "All you have heard about Old Narnia is true. It is not the land of men. It is the country of Aslan, the country of the Walking Trees and Visible Naiads, of Fauns and Satyrs, of Dwarfs and Giants, of the gods and the Centaurs, of Talking Beasts."[12]

Though these sound like fairy-tale characters, Dr. Cornelius assures Caspian that they are real. Narnia was once filled with such amazing creatures. Caspian must therefore surround himself with trustworthy, like-minded folk who also believe—creatures such as the fearless Trumpkin, the dwarf who leads the newly re-turned Pevensie clan to him, and, of course, Reepi-cheep, the valiant mouse, whose tail becomes a tale in itself during the story's climax. Peter, Susan, Edmund, and Lucy must sort out on short notice why and how they have suddenly been brought back to Narnia—and, upon understanding their mission and whom to trust, how they can gain the confidence of the agnostics to whom they must entrust Narnia's future.

In *Prince Caspian* we learn that one's vantage point is crucial and that one is responsible for both what and how one sees. On their second trip to Narnia, Peter and com-pany find Narnia in disarray—their once-splendid castle in ruins, their would-be friends discouraged, and its citizens unaware or outwardly doubtful that there has ever been a golden age in which Narnia prospered under Aslan's wise rule. The children's new quest—to restore the rightful King to his throne and his subjects to faith in Aslan—requires new resolve and a good memory for what Aslan has already taught them. They must piece to-gether the facts of their predicament and help Caspian convince and lead his subjects to recovery of their na-tional identity and faith as Narnians. The locals have no more reason to believe the children than they do the old stories. The children must again courageously prove themselves.

It is interesting to note the difference in temperament between the Sons of Adam and Daughters of Eve and those who belong to Narnia. The children once came as seemingly uninvited guests into Aslan's world, whereas the Narnians' birthright is peaceful living in the light of Cair Paravel. The Pevensie clan returns to Narnia with prior experience of fulfilled prophecy and a fresh awareness of Aslan's call. They are devastated by what has befallen the Narnians—Old Narnia is the only Narnia they know. The contemporary Narnians are diffident, and their bewilderment inhibits their ability to distinguish fact from falsehood. They must fathom their confusion, perplexity, anxiety, and ignorance about their origins and their destiny. They must resolve their profound ambiguity about the stories they are told and the stories they tell themselves, and then decide what to believe.

Truths don't lose their value or validity because they are old. This important maxim governs the whole of the Chronicles, and it is especially relevant here. The validity and truth of a statement is not determined by the time of its origin. In the Chronicles, Lewis fictionally debunks the "chronological snobbery" that he personally faced and defeated. He also describes this key event of his intellectual and spiritual liberation in *Surprised by Joy*.

Dr. Cornelius, Caspian, Trumpkin, and Reepicheep must all fight their skepticism in order to accept the truth of the old belief that Aslan exists and that Narnia's future is dependent on this ancient knowledge. Life for all of us is *in medias res;* we don't get to choose the moment in which we will enter the world, nor what conversations, ideas, victories, and defeats will have preceded or will succeed us. We have only the "now," and we must piece together the puzzle of our lives moment by moment. To accomplish this, valor alone does not suffice. Without a compass of faith and a community of believers, it is a daunting, perhaps impossible, task. New Narnia needs Old Narnia, and both rest on the foundation of Aslan's justice and the fellowship of those who embrace it.

Lucy and her siblings rely on the lessons learned and the character built during their earlier encounters with Aslan, and carry on his work in his seeming absence. They must be rational but not rationalistic, trusting but not naive, and courageous but not reckless. Lucy now has Edmund at her side, and both are willing to see with their hearts as Lucy's vision of Aslan's approach draws them forward. Their valor shows that we can trust Aslan to be who he was yesterday, is today, and will be forever, which is the supreme message of *Prince Caspian*. Reepicheep, the chivalrous mouse who takes a more central role in *The Voyage of the "Dawn Treader,"* understands this and proves that strength and courage are not measured by an individual's stature but by the size of his or her heart.

In *Prince Caspian*, we frankly confront the consequences of lost perspective and, worse, of lost faith and trust among friends. To assume the throne, Caspian must take to heart and act upon the lessons he received from Dr. Cornelius. The stories of Old Narnia must be handed down faithfully from generation to generation, for without them, Narnia will cease to exist. Throughout the tale, Caspian develops his understanding of how his father was murdered and the personal risk required of him in confronting evil. The Sons of Adam and Daughters of Eve are comforted and emboldened by the promise of new adventures in the company of old friends; their faith in Aslan is unshaken, though his timing may differ from theirs. The treacherous King Miraz, family member but usurper of the throne, can finally trust no one, not even his own guards. By contrast, Narnia teaches us that good character begets great friendships and shows us how to extend and nurture them. It is not so for corrupt and conniving despots.

These lessons of *Prince Caspian* provide an interesting link to the last several chapters of Lewis's autobiography, *Surprised by Joy*. There, Lewis explores the confusion and clarity of his own life as he weaves the threads of his past into a tapestry that reveals his discoveries about heritage, faith, hope, and destiny. Like Caspian, Lewis must sort out truth from falsehood, friendship from mere companionship, and ultimate joy from temporary pleasure or comfort. He has to read his life story with the help of insightful peers and mentors in order to embrace his true self. While there was no single Dr. Cornelius in his life, he did have Chesterton, MacDonald, Barfield, and Tolkien to help lead him home.

The dramatic climax of the story is not the victory over King Miraz in battle but the discovery of King Caspian's true lineage—he, too, is a Son of Adam, or he would not be qualified to reign in Narnia. In a poignant moment that epitomizes the humility of a true leader, Aslan asks the triumphant Caspian if he now feels ready to become king.

"'I—I don't think I do, Sir,' said Caspian. 'I'm only a kid.'"

To his surprise, Aslan replies, "If you had felt yourself sufficient, it would have been a proof that you were not."[13] Caspian needed to know the limits of his own powers and when to rely on others—especially Aslan—to win the day.

THE SINGLE STREAM:
JILL POLE IN *THE SILVER CHAIR*

The Silver Chair is third in the "Caspian Triad." Like the two preceding novels, *Prince Caspian* and *The Voyage of the "Dawn Treader*," it revolves around the kingly rule of Caspian. The stories also have in common what is sometimes called "the initiation theme," that is, a tale in which the growth and grooming of a young man or woman into adulthood is central to the plot.

There are, in fact, many characters, both human and

Narnian, who are initiated during these three stories, beginning with Prince Caspian. In the first two works, the initiates include Lucy, Edmund, Eustace, and Reepicheep. In *The Silver Chair*, the company grows to include Prince Rilian and Jill Pole, the latest human to journey to Narnia. Like Lucy and Susan before her, Jill begins as a weaker person in the shadow of a male companion and then emerges second-to-none as a courageous and decisive young woman, formidable in faith and dynamic leadership.

Jill and Eustace are schoolmates at Experiment House, an institution that Lewis has already skewered in *The Voyage of the "Dawn Treader."* As a modern, progressive school, it is trendy and superficial, actually teaching pupils very little about the world in which they live. Jill, like Eustace, must travel to Narnia for a real education, as demonstrated by the very events that send them both there.

Chased by bullies, Eustace suggests to Jill that they try somehow to get to Narnia. Jill has never heard of Narnia and needs some encouragement to believe in it. Eustace asks, sheepishly, "Are you good at believing things? I mean things that everyone here would laugh at?"

"I've never had the chance," Jill replies, "but I think I would be."[14]

So far so good—Jill's openness is the key to her transformation. Eustace suggests that they try magic, shorthand for something much more wonderful, as Eustace points out that the only way to get to Narnia is to call upon Aslan.

"Aslan, Aslan, Aslan," they implore, the heart cry of all who need to be saved.[15]

As the bullies close in, Eustace and Jill reach the edge of a cliff. Here Jill selfishly tries to prove that she has no fear of heights and inadvertently causes Eustace to fall. Next she finds herself blown into Narnia by Aslan, apparently alone. To prepare Jill for the mission he has in mind for her and Eustace, Aslan must first teach Jill something about himself and about Narnia. Before she can rejoin Eustace and embark on their adventure, she needs to learn that relationships are built upon experiential, not experimental, knowledge. She must trust in individuals and, most of all, trust in him. This is her first lesson in courage.

> "*Do* you eat girls?" she said.
>
> "I have swallowed up girls and boys, women and men, kings and emperors, cities and realms," said the Lion. . . .
>
> "I daren't come and drink," said Jill.
>
> "Then you will die of thirst," said the Lion.
>
> "Oh dear!" said Jill, coming a step nearer. "I suppose I must go and look for another stream then."
>
> "There is no other stream," said the Lion.[16]

Jill's first reaction, like the Pevensies in *The Lion, the Witch, and the Wardrobe*, is to be cautious in approaching this talking—and perhaps stalking?—Lion. Who can blame her? And yet, if she is to satisfy her thirst, she must resist her fears and come closer to Aslan, for he is the source of her very life. Aslan makes no promises; he is not safe, having "swallowed" kings and realms, but he is *good*. As a good King, he prepares his people for their lifelong service to him by teaching them proper reverence.

When she finally faces Aslan, he asks about Eustace's whereabouts, and she has to confess that she does not know—she caused his fall because she was showing off. Thus chastened, she listens to an astonishing tale: It was not they who were calling to him, but the other way around. "You would not have called to me unless I had been calling to you," Aslan tells Jill.[17] We may think that a life circumstance is accidental or self-engineered, and the almosts and close calls of life lead us to believe that some part of life, large or small, is "chance" or "the breaks," but Aslan demolishes those notions.

Jill learns that they have been drafted for a mission of the utmost importance—the discovery and rescue of a lost prince, or their death in trying. Like Moses when confronted by God at the burning bush, Jill offers all sorts of excuses for why she is not up to the task. Undaunted, Aslan enlists Jill and explains the four signs by which she can chart their progress in finding Prince Rilian:

1. Eustace will meet and greet an old friend.
2. They must leave Narnia and head north to the ruined city of ancient giants.
3. They must observe the writing on a stone in that ruined city and obey its directions.
4. They will know the lost prince they seek because he will be the first person in their travels to ask them to do something in Aslan's name.

In asking Jill to memorize these signs and to follow them precisely, Aslan echoes a biblical exhortation from Deuteronomy: "Say them to yourself when you wake in the morning and when you lie down at night, and when you wake in the middle of the night. And whatever strange things may happen to you, let nothing turn your mind from following the signs."[18]

The parallel in our world is explicit—God told the Israelites to remember what he had taught them through the law of Moses:

> *Hear, O Israel: The LORD our God, the LORD is one. Love the LORD your God with all your heart and with all your soul and with all your strength. These commandments that I give you today are to be upon your hearts. Impress them on your children. Talk about them when*

you sit at home and when you walk along the road, when you lie down and when you get up. Tie them as symbols on your hands and bind them on your foreheads. Write them on the doorframes of your houses and on your gates.

DEUTERONOMY 6:4-9

Lewis reminds us of this refrain as a way of drawing attention to the necessity of following Aslan's counsel; when the friends depart from the four signs, not only do they lose their way—they also lose heart. Jill and Eustace are thus called upon to treat the signs like Scripture, memorizing them and sharing them with each other throughout their journey. It is upon her careful listening to and conveying of these signs, first to Eustace, and then to their other companions, that the success of their mission depends. And, of course, it is this task and Jill's muddling of it (in forgetting the signs and their significance) that gives the plot of *The Silver Chair* its twists and turns.

The Silver Chair is unique among the seven Narnia tales in focusing so intently on this one theme. In order to defeat the enemy's most powerful weapons, all doubt, skepticism, and hopelessness must be conquered. This happens, as it does for Prince Caspian, by remembering who one is and by recognizing to whom one belongs. Aslan called Eustace and Jill into Narnia because he knew their character. They, in turn, need to understand him and his character and become as strong and faithful as he.

POISE UNDER PRESSURE:
PUDDLEGLUM IN *THE SILVER CHAIR*

The Silver Chair has many of the distinctive features we have come to expect, and that Lewis loved, in fairy tales: knights, wicked queens, shape-shifters, giants, mysterious strangers, cast spells, and a demanding series of riddles to be solved in order to locate the lost captive. The Underland, the subterranean world into which Puddleglum, Jill, and Eustace fall, echoes much ancient literature, most notably that of the Greek philosopher Plato, whose "Allegory of the Cave" is partly its inspiration. In Plato's story, cave dwellers can see only the shadows of the real world on the cave wall and long to know the real world through their distorted view. The Queen of the Underland reverses Plato's allegory and attempts to defeat Puddleglum and company by convincing them that Narnia is the illusion and that the shadows in her world are the true reality.

Perhaps the most arresting fairy-tale element is found in the adventurers' stay in Harfang, where they are the honored guests of the ancient city's gentle giants. Along the way, the three travelers have encountered a beautiful lady in green accompanied by a silent black knight; she encourages them to attend the annual autumn feast. Despite Puddleglum's wariness, Eustace and Jill imagine a sumptuous menu and safe quarters. It takes them little time to realize that they are afforded cordiality and hospitality simply because they are the main course for the feast! As in "Hansel and Gretel" or "Jack and the Beanstalk," the threat of being someone's dinner always motivates our heroes!

Escaping this dire fate leads the trio into even more peril as they fall through a tunnel into the underworld in which Prince Rilian is imprisoned by enchantment. Their successful fight against this enchantment frees themselves as well as Rilian from the powers of deception and fear and forms the climax to the most intense and rousing personal battle to be found in the Chronicles of Narnia.

Still, *The Silver Chair* is most notable for how Jill and Eustace, despite their hairbreadth escapes and heroic actions, are upstaged by the precisely and completely realized character of one of Lewis's most memorable Narnians. You know him. He always finds the dark lining in the silver cloud. He's never met a situation he couldn't be gloomy about, and if there are those ready to be optimistic about anything, he has the perfect word to quell their hopes. It's a different kind of valor.

It's Puddleglum the Marsh-wiggle, of course, the most unlikely hero in *The Silver Chair*. He is one of Lewis's most beloved characters precisely because he is the obverse of so many of the creatures that populate Narnia's landscape. He is not dashing, full of ambition, or a clever strategist. He is as much Hobbit as Narnian—a reluctant and pessimistic hero at best, yet hands down the most interesting and humorous of all the sidekicks Lewis created to accompany his human characters on their adventures. His only rival, perhaps, is Reepicheep, the valiant mouse of *Prince Caspian* and *The Voyage of the "Dawn Treader."*

Puddleglum has two of the qualities that Lewis prized most among his friends and colleagues: absolute loyalty (he is dutiful to a fault) and a profound belief in Providence—that nothing happens merely by accident. His loyalty and perseverance are based on a deeper hope that finds its center in Aslan and the signs he has entrusted to Jill; the friends' discovery of these qualities is crucial to the adventures of *The Silver Chair*. These signs become the fulcrum for the fulfilling of their quest to find the missing prince who must become king to avenge his mother's death. Without their loyalty to one another and their trust in Aslan's benevolent care, none of them would survive the treacherous journeys through the Wild Waste Lands of the North, the House of Harfang, or the Underland, where the prince remains imprisoned by his mother's murderer, the Queen of the Underland.

Eventually, the children's own belief in Narnia and their faith in Aslan falter, and their courage is drained by the Queen's insistence that Narnia is a myth and that there is "no Overworld, no sky, no sun, no Aslan."[19] But the steadfast Puddleglum, under torture, declares that he will believe in Narnia and live as a Narnian—even if he has only dreamed that there is such a place as Narnia and such a lion as Aslan.

"I'm a chap who always liked to know the worst and then put the best face I can on it. So I won't deny any of what you said. But there's one thing more to be said, even so. Suppose we *have* only dreamed, or made up, all those things—trees and grass and sun and moon and stars and Aslan himself. Suppose we have. Then all I can say is that, in that case, the made-up things seem a good deal more important than the real ones. . . . That's why I'm going to stand by the play-world. I'm on Aslan's side even if there isn't any Aslan to lead it. I'm going to live as like a Narnian as I can even if there isn't any Narnia."[20]

This strong declaration of faith is the measure that defeats their adversary and brings the adventurers through their trials unscathed. Puddleglum's spiritual courage is the hallmark of true Narnian spirit. One's self-confidence may be broken under challenge, but the resilient Narnian will reach out in trust to Aslan in order to withstand threat and harassment.

Puddleglum's apparent pessimism is revealed under fire to be a hardheaded realism born of true faith. His defiant trust in Aslan and in what it means to be a Narnian saves the day. Puddleglum's surface pessimism is, of course, exaggerated; by no means does Lewis suggest that we adopt the Marsh-wiggle's cranky disposition as a way of muddling through life's challenges. But Puddleglum's caution and gloom never descend to cynicism. Rather, his eccentric charm reflects Lewis's admiration for those whose true character—built on the rock of faith and the thirst for what is real—shows through in times of crisis. Puddleglum's values are shown to be in line with those of all true Narnians. Good will triumph over evil if we do not mistake evil for good, or evil's messengers as trustworthy allies of Aslan.

When their identity as friends of Aslan and loyal subjects of Narnia is ridiculed, the children, armed by Puddleglum's unbreakable trust, stand against the enslaving lies and deceptions. While there certainly are physical menaces to be faced, the gravest danger the children and Puddleglum must overcome is the temptation to renounce all that they hold dear. Aslan need not appear to fight their battles for them as long as they retain their trust in what he has told them and embrace their destiny as his agents for truth and righteousness. In the end, Puddleglum's refrain, "There *are* no accidents. Our guide is Aslan," is the profound exclamation point, the masterful counterstatement to the Queen of the Underland's wicked lies.[21]

GRACE MEETS HUMILITY:
DIGORY KIRKE AND POLLY PLUMMER
IN *THE MAGICIAN'S NEPHEW*

As we have already noted, *The Magician's Nephew* is the Narnia tale that Lewis completed last. It also contains the most poignant biographical parallel to Lewis's own life in the illness of his mother as depicted in *Surprised by Joy*. Since Lewis was working on both texts simultaneously, it is not surprising that the themes overlap. What is surprising is how delicately and effectively Lewis weaves this very personal episode from his life into the story without becoming maudlin or melodramatic. The Chronicles of Narnia depict many absent or ailing parents, through evil treachery or the tribulations of life on either side of the Wardrobe. This theme is a staple of many children's adventure novels and fairy tales—certainly among those Lewis loved—and provides the background exposition that explains why the children are freely roaming, unchaperoned, in forests, glens, deserts, and foreign lands. How could they have such adventures unless Mom or Dad were otherwise occupied or missing? But in Narnia it is more than that. It reflects the author's own childhood loneliness, disaffection, and hurt—and the need for a benevolent Father to replace these absent guides and confidantes. Lewis knew that many readers would identify with characters whose home life mirrored his heartaches and sadness.

A person reading *The Magician's Nephew* can see how therapeutic it must have been for Lewis to revisit this traumatic incident from his life. His writing about it simultaneously affirmed its resolution in his soul and frankly dramatized how personal trials and losses can derail one's faith and hope. The point is not that Digory is an exact parallel created to exorcise demons in Lewis's personal life but that Lewis provides a way to fictionally explore the emotions and clouded judgments one is likely to experience under duress. There is a happy ending, but its conclusion is less poignant than the journey Digory takes to get there.

When we first meet Digory, his mother, Mabel, is seriously ill— perhaps dying. He and his mother have come to stay at the Ketterley house with his aunt and uncle because his father is away in India. Digory is depicted as a decent young man, not as given to priggish selfishness as Edmund or Eustace, but equally flawed by his inability to anticipate the consequences of his actions or to take counsel from the wiser Polly. By the story's end, Digory has begun the lifelong journey toward maturity that we see him complete in *The Last Battle* as Lord Digory.

Despite his mistakes, once Digory arrives in Narnia he never uses his quest to explore forbidden knowledge or to make himself rich, but only to find a way to save his mother. What Lewis's prayers as a young boy did not accomplish, Digory's trust in Aslan does. In his journey of faith, like all other Sons of Adam, Digory must first undergo a test that will prepare him for the greater challenges that lie ahead. Digory has already shown himself to be a young man of character by finding and rescuing Polly when Uncle Andrew has tricked her into wearing the magic ring.

Once he crosses over into the new world beyond

the woods, Digory becomes confused. Unlike Polly, whose spiritual instincts tell her when things are not right, Digory becomes enamored of the dying world, Charn, and eventually of Jadis. He must face himself squarely and realize the enormity of his misstep. That Digory takes responsibility for the rash act that freed Jadis to cause trouble in London and to bring real evil to Narnia is a tribute to his ability to listen and to learn from his shortcomings. He learns the grander lesson that laying down one's life for another is a source of joy and a route to the greater good, and Aslan entrusts him with the mission of retrieving the life-giving apple.

Avoiding the downfall of his ancient parents Adam and Eve in unlawfully eating from the tree of the knowledge of good and evil in the biblical story of Genesis, Digory resists Jadis's evil rhetoric and completes his mission faithfully. Digory's humility in recognizing Aslan's authority allows him to turn away from Jadis's suggestion to abandon Polly and steal an apple, despite the fact that his heart is breaking over his mother's impending death. The contrast between faith and faithlessness is captured in Aslan's explanation to Polly about Uncle Andrew's fate:

> "He thinks great folly, child," said Aslan. "This world is bursting with life for these few days because the song with which I called it into life still hangs in the air and rumbles in the ground. It will not be so

for long. But I cannot tell that to this old sinner, and I cannot comfort him, either; he has made himself unable to hear my voice. If I spoke to him, he would hear only growlings and roarings. Oh, Adam's sons, how cleverly you defend yourselves against all that might do you good!"[22]

What a dreadful thought—becoming deaf to God's voice through persistent disobedience and self-service. Because Digory trusted Aslan to do what was best, he was able to hear his voice, and Aslan's grace met Digory's humble heart. Through this intersection, his mother received her health again.

Polly is one of the most intrepid and spiritually astute characters in all of Narnia, and certainly as heroic and dynamic as Lucy Pevensie or Jill Pole. She is, in fact, the first human child to enter the Wood between the Worlds, and she is by far the best prepared for the adventures she experiences there.

With all valorous Narnians, Polly understands what is required of those who wish to follow this un-tame Lion. In the end—paraphrasing what guide George Macdonald tells the mystified Lewis who gropes for heavenly comprehension in *The Great Divorce*—there are two kinds of Narnians: those who say to Aslan, "thy will be done" and those to whom Aslan says, "thy will be done." It is a terrible thing to fall into the paws of a good Lion.

CHAPTER 4

VICTORY OVER VANITY:

Transformations and Revivals

"Oh, Aslan," said she, "it was kind of you to come."

"I have been here all the time," said he, "but you have just made me visible."

"Aslan!" said Lucy almost a little reproachfully. "Don't make fun of me.
As if anything I could do would make you visible!"

"It did," said Aslan. "Do you think I wouldn't obey my own rules?"[1]

THE VOYAGE OF THE "DAWN TREADER"

Vanity—as pride, conceit, arrogance, self-promotion, or excessive attention to appearance, and as "I'm better and smarter than you" because of my looks, money, GPA, parents, color, ethnic background, or political connections—is detrimental to our spiritual growth and injurious to our spiritual health. In Narnia, vanity will associate you with wicked queens, self-important princes and usurpers, stubborn and hopelessly egotistical talking beasts, and occasionally with the Sons of Adam and Daughters of Eve. To be vain is to be competitive, not only with one's fellow creatures and siblings but with God. Lewis places the sin of pride at the center of the human predicament in *Mere Christianity* and explores its impact:

> Now what you want to get clear is that Pride is *essentially* competitive—is competitive by its very nature—while the other vices are competitive only, so to speak, by accident. Pride gets no pleasure out of having something, only out of having more of it than the next man. We say that people are proud of being rich, or clever, or good-looking, but they are not. They are proud of being richer, or cleverer, or better-looking than others. If every one else became equally rich, or clever, or good-looking there would be nothing to be proud about. It is the comparison

that makes you proud: the pleasure of being above the rest.[2]

Pride can come in small or large doses, and it can be conquered with the help of those who lovingly speak the truth to us. It is only fatal in those who fail to reach the end of themselves in humility before the great King Aslan.

The peril of pride is in its subtlety and in its creeping, incremental grasp of our self-image and point of view. We slip into vanity whenever we cease to see the world through the eyes of others, of even one other, and when our perspective declares that we hold—and deserve—dominion. Vanity is at the heart of every betrayal, lie, seizure of power, and act of vengeance or treachery; its essential nature is what Lewis, in defining the character of Satan in Milton's *Paradise Lost*, calls "incessant autobiography."

> Satan's monomaniac concern with himself and his supposed rights and wrongs is a necessity of the Satanic predicament. Certainly, he has no choice. He chose to have no choice. He has wished to "be himself," and to be in himself and for himself, and his wish has been granted. The Hell he carries with him is, in one sense, a Hell of infinite boredom. Satan . . . is interesting to read about; but Milton makes plain the blank uninterestingness of being Satan.[3]

Our hope is that, when convinced of our vanity and pride, we may find *transformation*, the redemption and direction of our gifts and aptitudes into heavenly endeavor, and *revival*, the sustaining and animating power to remain focused and committed, which can come only through encounter with the One who created us to serve him and others by finding our true selves. In the characters we consider in this chapter, we find Aslan dynamically at work transforming and redeeming his creation.

AND THEY ALMOST DESERVED IT: EUSTACE, CASPIAN, AND LUCY IN *THE VOYAGE OF THE "DAWN TREADER"*

Early in his precocious childhood, Clive Staples Lewis transformed himself into "Jacksie," the name by which he insisted that his family and friends call him. Later, his name evolved into "Jack," a name as unpretentious, down to earth, and homespun as the characters in the nursery rhymes and tales Lewis loved from his cradle forward, such as "Jack and the Beanstalk" and "Jack, Be Nimble." "Jack" also stands in vivid contrast to "Clive Staples," an aristocratic, smug-sounding name, especially to children's ears. When he named the spoiled and selfish brat Eustace Clarence Scrubb in *The Voyage of the "Dawn Treader,"* Lewis chose a combination of names that conveys a sense of conceited self-satisfaction.

In the scene in which Eustace is first introduced,

Lewis draws attention to the arrogance represented by the boy's name: "There was a boy called Eustace Clarence Scrubb, and he almost deserved it."[4] Eustace deserved his reputation as a boy full of himself, committed to his own pleasure and preeminence, and decidedly immune to adventures that would test his boyhood bravery or augment his strengths. His idea of a fun holiday was getting the opportunity to boss and bully his cousins, the Pevensies. Lewis unabashedly presents Eustace as a young man compromised by his progressive education and prohibited by his ego from enjoying nature or the companionship of others. Eustace enjoyed books "if they . . . had pictures of grain elevators or of fat foreign children doing exercises in model schools" and he liked animals, "especially beetles, if they were dead and pinned on a card."[5]

What Eustace lacks most, in other words, is imagination. He loves teasing his cousins about their stories of Narnia. Eustace believed "they were making it all up" and since, according to the narrator, "he was quite incapable of making anything up himself, he did not approve of that."[6] For Lewis, as we know, imagination is the safe haven of childhood. Even in the midst of turmoil, it can provide grand and glorious encounters with creatures and adventures that ennoble the spirit, taking one to the limits of reality and beyond, to the sublime and the transcendent. Everyone hopes that there is a heaven and seeks Aslan's country, even if one's head denies it. Imagination is seeing with the heart, seeing one-self in true relationship to the universe one inhabits.

Narnia is a place that not only permits, but requires exercise of the imagination. Peter, Edmund, Susan, and Lucy have—with Professor Kirke's help—happily jour-neyed to Narnia with imagination (and logic!) as tools of encounter and triumph. In *The Voyage of the "Dawn Treader,"* Eustace needs a direct encounter with Aslan in order to see, for the first time, how his ingrown char-acter and spirit have shriveled his soul. Before Eustace can be heroic—the purpose for which every Son of Adam and Daughter of Eve come into Narnia—he must face who he is and how he has been shaped by his envi-ronment into a horror and a mockery of what young boys can and should be.

Few of us, looking in the mirror, see what others see; certainly we do not see as God sees. We have a fallen tendency to see someone smarter, someone more clever, dashing, and charming. Or we may have the opposite problem—seeing ourselves as worse than we really are while hoping that someone will tell us differently. Either stance is a form of vanity—a way of calling attention to ourselves to prove our greater worth or worthlessness. Regardless, chances are that we do not see the reflection of a dragon when we look in the mirror.

Dragons are legendary hoarders and misers that collect precious jewels and gold and protect them with their fiery breath. Eustace was a dragon—a selfish miser of emotion and friendship—long before he visibly became one, just as Edmund had a traitorous heart long before the White Witch enticed him with Turkish Delight. Eustace learned heroism only when he divested himself of all the pretenses and supposed superiority that his name and education represented. By morphing him into a dragon, Aslan demonstrates that character is more than skin deep. It is soul deep—and Aslan's "undragoning" of Eustace is symbolic of repentance and restoration. Only when Eustace saw his dragon soul, dreadful as it was, could he finally see the Eustace he had become, and this enabled him to embrace the Eustace he was called to be. His generally sour attitude, laziness, and greed led him, as it leads us, into the dragon's lair. If we succumb to temptation, we become what we envision, what we dwell on. That is why vanity is so seductive. It becomes a permanent habit unless we repent. The persistent pursuit of anything short of absolute joy leads to ruin and sentences the soul to jealousy and despair.

Seen initially through the eyes of the cocky and self-righteous Eustace, the crew of King Caspian's ship seems a ragtag collection. The odd and vaguely disreputable sailors are led by a mouthy mouse, whom Eustace insults by treating him as a performing animal of the kind he has seen in his own land. Reepicheep's bravery, chivalry, and authority are unsettling to Eustace, as they should be. In Narnia, mice can talk and be chivalrous—

as can beavers, wolves, fauns, and lions. Shock is a common response upon first entering Narnia.

Because Eustace has disdained his cousins' recounting of their earlier exploits in Narnia, he has no context for understanding who any of these strange folk are, and he doesn't know how he could possibly have ended up in the middle of a sea. Unsure of himself and wary of his new companions, he can think only of his own selfish comforts. Before his "undragoning," his eyes were the only ones he could bear to look through. Thanks to Aslan, his poison did not infect the rest of the crew.

Lewis quickly establishes that this adventure is not primarily about personal advancement but about a national emergency and that King Caspian still has some growing up of his own to do. The crew sets out to find King Caspian's father's friends—the seven Lords banished from Narnia by the evil usurper, King Miraz, as related in *Prince Caspian*. They have been called to complete the history of Narnia that Dr. Cornelius had long ago shared with Caspian, to write its final pages so that the lost stories could be preserved and told again and again. The crew must travel toward the Utter East—beyond the seas that Narnians would normally have encountered. Reepicheep is the same brave and persevering spiritual warrior that we met in *Prince Caspian*. His size belies his depth of character and courage, and he will not be deterred from his desire to enter Aslan's country, where his final joy awaits him. Like

Shangri La, the Utter East is a mystical place en route to Aslan's country, and the timing for the journey is in Aslan's hands, as both Reepicheep and Caspian discover.

To finish their mission, they must remain united as a crew of stalwart adventurers willing to sail unknown seas. It is not always smooth sailing, especially when Caspian announces, "Friends, . . . we have now fulfilled the quest on which you embarked. . . . I am going with Reepicheep to see the World's End."[7]

The crew reacts immediately—this is abdication and desertion on the high seas, and there is no worse crime. The King of Narnia has made a vain and selfish decision, as all his crew agrees. To address Caspian's sudden bout of overweening vanity, the faithful, valiant mouse must rebuke his King's unexpected stubbornness, reversing the tactics of Ulysses' sail mates when Ulysses desires to hear the Siren's song on his voyage:

> "You are the King of Narnia. You break faith with all your subjects, and especially with Trumpkin, if you do not return. You shall not please yourself with adventures as if you were a private person. And if your Majesty will not hear reason, it will be the truest loyalty of every man on board to follow me in disarming and binding you till you come to your senses."[8]

Edmund warns Caspian that his sailing on with Reepicheep would be equivalent to listening to the Siren's song like Ulysses and inviting death—not just for Caspian but for his entire crew. Reepicheep's single-minded pursuit of joy, his final journey to Aslan's country, is accomplished not by putting it ahead of the other needs of the crew or the challenges of the mission but by laying his life on the line for their common success. Only by following Reepicheep's example and embracing the greater good (and being reminded of the Queen-in-waiting for him at home!) can Caspian find himself privileged to enter into the glorious heritage that will include his sons and daughters.

From island to island, the crew members—including Edmund, Lucy, and Eustace—are called upon to step out in faith, trusting not in what they can see (sometimes they can't see anything at all) but in what their hearts tell them. Appearances can be deceiving, and the children and the crew must learn and relearn that Aslan is in control and that all their destinies are in his kingly and compassionate paws. It is only by putting first things—the good of Narnia—at the forefront of their quest that each is enabled to understand and fulfill his or her individual destiny. This thread is central to Lewis's worldview, to what he called the "doctrine of first and second things," which, in turn, is a paraphrase of Jesus' call to seek first the kingdom of God.[9] For Lewis, by setting first the most noble goals and character traits, one can more reliably and directly also achieve the lesser goals and desires that otherwise would tempt one to depart from the greater good. "Aim at Heaven and you will get earth 'thrown in'; aim at earth and you will get neither."[10]

The usually noble Lucy undergoes some serious character tests for the first time in her Narnia adventures when she is tempted by her perusal of the Magician's Book to perform many spells that will be only to her own advantage, not for her spiritual development or the mission of the crew. She seeks knowledge of others and of the future that is not hers to have, for it could serve no useful purpose in her life. If successful, these spells would only increase her need to compound them with other spells to maintain her competitive edge on beauty, intelligence, wealth, or glory. The temptation comes in the vain ambition to place oneself on a higher plane than someone else. Her real task is to develop the true and enduring beauty of inner goodness, but only a vision of the Lion can turn her vanity aside. It rises up when she quickly utters ("all in a hurry, for fear her mind would change") the words of a spell that will allow her to eavesdrop on her school friends to find out what they really think of her.[11]

In the epigraph to this chapter, Lucy expresses a false modesty about her relationship with Aslan, and he gently but firmly confronts her with this and her spell casting by pointing out his own consistency: "Do you think I wouldn't obey my own rules?"[12] Lucy, too, has rules. She has a conscience with which she is wrestling throughout the episode, revealing that even those of generally good character must be on guard against temptations they are not yet strong enough to withstand. "Doing them in a hurry" before we can resist is not a wise solution. Aslan scolds Lucy and calls upon her to recognize this vanity for what it is and to acknowledge that "spying on people by magic is the same as spying on them in any other way." He tells her that she has misjudged her friend. "She is weak, but she loves you."

Stung by this revelation, Lucy still pleads for further forbidden knowledge to salve her conscience: "Have I spoiled everything? Do you mean we would have gone on being friends if it hadn't been for this . . . and now we never shall."

Aslan provides the only wise answer possible. "Child," said Aslan, "did I not explain to you once before that no one is ever told what would have happened?"[13]

Somehow, in Lucy's fragile state, she believes that knowing whether or not some consequence of her wrongdoing is insurmountable would comfort her. In fact, it is just an extension of her vain attempt at self-justification. For all her spiritual sensitivity and strength Lucy does have weaknesses, and these lead to insecurity about what her friends think and to an inferiority complex about her own looks. Only when thwarted by Aslan's gaze does she realize that her self-worth does not rest in physical appearance or insider information but in being accepted for who she is as Aslan's chosen one.

Toward the end of this tale, the cosmic Aslan returns. He is both Lamb and Lion, Savior and Sovereign, appearing in a scene reminiscent of the disciples' heartrending encounter with Jesus at the end of the Gospel of John.

"Come and have breakfast," said the Lamb, offering them roasted fish.

"Please, Lamb," said Lucy, still sorrowful upon saying farewell to Reepicheep, "is this the way to Aslan's country?"

Cryptically, the Lamb tells them, "Not for you. . . . For you the door into Aslan's country is from your own world."

Shocked at this revelation, Edmund blurts out, "Is there a way into Aslan's country from our world too?"

He is met with an equal shocker as the Lamb transforms into a tawny gold Lion who proclaims, "There is a way into my country from all the worlds."

Awestruck, but sensing the ultimacy of their conversation after Aslan tells them that he is sending them home, Lucy plaintively begs Aslan to tell her when they can return. Aslan must then comfort the two remaining Pevensies, who will not be returning to Narnia again.

"Dearest, . . . you and your brother will never come back to Narnia."[14]

Told that they are too old and must remain closer to their world, Lucy is, understandably, inconsolable:

"It isn't Narnia, you know," sobbed Lucy. "It's *you*. We shan't meet *you* there. And how can we live, never meeting you?"

"But you shall meet me, dear one," said Aslan.

"Are—are you there too, Sir?" said Edmund.

"I am," said Aslan. "But there I have another name. You must learn to know me by that name. This was the very reason why you were brought to Narnia, that by knowing me here for a little, you may know me better there."[15]

In this emotional scene, Aslan reveals the reason for their journey, and ours, too. There comes a time when, painful though it is, the transformations and revivals have done their work, and we are to take our place in leading others to him. Our own pilgrimage to Aslan's country is then well under way.

STUBBORNNESS IS AS STUBBORNNESS DOES: SHASTA AND ARAVIS IN *THE HORSE AND HIS BOY*

Lewis set six of the Chronicles within Narnia's boundaries, but *The Horse and His Boy* takes us to two bordering lands, Archenland and Calormen, for its main action. The tale is set within the years that Peter, Edmund, Susan, and Lucy rule as kings and queens of Narnia at Cair Paravel; so chronologically, its action takes place between the events of *The Lion, the Witch, and the Wardrobe* and *Prince Caspian*. It is "back story," the recounting of a side tale that helps to form the backdrop for what else has been happening in Narnia. We don't need to know any of the characters or situations covered here to understand the other Narnia tales, but we love encountering them, all the same. They help us to understand Mr. Beaver's comment that "Aslan is not to be tied down," since he has "many countries" to visit and rule.[16] The story is told partly to provide a profound contrast between Narnian ethics and those of the cultures outside its boundaries. It provides a new vantage point on Aslan's benevolent care for all his creation, even for those who do not know or trust him.

Only by being in the midst of unfamiliar territory with its geographical, cultural, and emotional contrasts can we fully understand ourselves or others. Lewis wants us to see Narnia afresh, but indirectly, through the eyes of Shasta and Aravis as they emerge from their bondage in Calormen. What a culture believes determines how its citizens treat one another, and the deity they worship creates them in the image of that deity. The Calormenes refer to their demonic god, Tash, as "the inexorable, the irresistible," whose traits explicitly contrast with those of Aslan, the benevolent and caring Creator of Narnia.[17]

Archenland is Narnia's smaller, southern neighbor, a country of gentle hills and snow-peaked mountains, whose relations with Narnia are cordial. Calormen is still farther south and separated from Archenland by a vast desert. Its capital city is Tashbaan, a name with Arabian overtones. There are allusions to Calormen in *The Voyage of the "Dawn Treader"* as a market for the slave trade in the Cane Islands—the first disturbing suggestion that there could be a culture in Aslan's world, albeit outside the precincts of Narnia, in which slavery and class-based prejudice are woven into the social fabric and not merely the decree of a despot. Possibly, Lewis coined the name of the country from the Latin word *calor*, which means heat or warmth. Thus, Calormen might describe a country of "people from a warm land."

The Calormenes are quickly identified as imperialistic followers of the demanding and malevolent god Tash, whose theology will be discussed in chapter 6. In following Tash, the Calormenes practice a religion of slavery, promote a class-based society, and do not disguise their desire to enslave the free northern kingdoms and become rulers of all. In Calormen, the highborn and the lowborn all observe their stations in life; they do not enjoy the egalitarian social order found in Narnia. In Tash's land, there are no native talking beasts, and the animals of Calormen are treated as mere property. By contrast, the talking beasts of Narnia enjoy full citizenship with all other creatures. As Shasta learns, talking horses are never mounted and ridden, except in battle. They most certainly are not enslaved to perform mundane tasks for human beings!

The Horse and His Boy is in some ways the only "indigenous" Narnia tale; that is, focused on Narnian characters throughout without relying primarily on intervention from Sons of Adam or Daughters of Eve. It is also told within the context of a storytelling tradition that Lewis wished to emulate because of his love of *The Arabian Nights,* whence he found the name of his Lion King, Aslan. It is also the only plot among the Chronicles built primarily around the exploits of a strong heroine from start to finish. Aravis's desire to escape a forced marriage parallels Queen Susan's need to avoid an unwise marriage to the Tisroc's son, Prince Rabadash. One of the talking beasts, Bree, gets top billing in this story, with more than a supporting role. From the title forward, Lewis undercuts our expectations and draws attention to the several reversals in this plot.

The Horse and His Boy resonates with themes as old as Homer's *Odyssey* and as modern as Mark Twain's *The Prince and the Pauper.* For example, a mystery shrouds the birth and early life of the hero. When he discovers who his real father is, there is a surprising revelation of his true homeland. The plot is embellished with scenes of mistaken identity and the deliberate switching of places between a peasant or slave and one with a more noble heritage. The tale is thus notable for twists and turns in which the reader knows more than the characters do about their destinies, which creates a different kind of anticipation. We read not so much to find out what will happen as to see how the main characters will react when they discover what we already know.

Aslan is present, but he plays a subtle role in the plot. By the end of the tale, of course, we can see that he has been behind the scenes, shaping the progress of the young protagonists from the beginning. Thematically, Lewis is foregrounding the theological principle of Providence through a picture of God's heavenly care and protection that can be seen only in retrospect. Ironically, the two sets of fugitives, who move in fear of the roar of hungry lions, are unaware until the climax of the tale that the roar is Aslan's, as he protects and guides their journey. When the undisguised Aslan meets Shasta later in the story as the King of Narnia, he reveals the circumstances in which he was, in fact, right by Shasta's side, showing him the way home. No wonder Shasta had from the beginning found himself "very interested in everything that lay to the north."[18] He exclaims, "I've been longing to go to the North all my life."[19] This desire, a pointer to his true country, resonates deep in his heart as a gift from Aslan. Bree also frequently whinnies, "Narnia and the North!"

In this longing, Shasta shares an experience with Lewis that we noted in chapter 1. As a young man, Lewis was captivated by a melancholy but pleasurable feeling he called "Northernness," an affection and aspiration stirred by the Norse mythology he had read.[20] Therein, he found an early intimation of the longing for his "own country" that he identifies as joy in *Surprised by Joy* and later associates with heaven. The continuing journey of Shasta and Bree is thus motivated by the persistent inner sense that they, too, belong somewhere else—that servitude is not their natural state and that Calormen is not their home. Somewhere there is a realm that truly satisfies their longing, an elusive experience of joy that carries them beyond the dimensions of this world. Lewis explored this phenomenon in *Surprised by Joy* as well as in his sermons:

> Do what they will, we remain conscious of a desire which no natural happiness will satisfy. But is there any reason to suppose that reality offers any satisfaction to it? . . . A man's physical hunger does not prove that that man will get any bread; he may die of starvation on a raft in the Atlantic. But surely a man's hunger does prove that he comes of a race which repairs its body by eating and inhabits a world where eatable substances exist. In the same way, though I do not believe (I wish I did) that my desire for Paradise proves that I shall enjoy it, I think it a pretty good indication that such a thing exists and that some men will.[21]

This kind of inner vision provides Shasta and Bree with a powerful catalyst for their overland search. Overhearing himself being bargained for as a slave to a

Calormen warlord, Shasta bolts and, apparently by chance, encounters a talking horse, a free beast from Narnia. In their encounter, he discerns for the first time that he may not be living in his real home after all—a thought that is liberating long before he is actually free. The knowledge that he may be more than he seems to be, that he might be a nobleman's son, is an exhilarating and energizing fantasy. If only it were true! What new possibilities this could mean for him and his future! But it is Lewis's genius to parallel the intertwined destinies of this unusual pair with those of still another unlikely runaway duo: Hwin and Aravis.

Aravis is everything Shasta is not: aristocratic and brash, self-possessed and secure in her identity. This young lady has the best of Calormen culture: prestige, riches, status—everything but freedom. She is ostensibly escaping a forced marriage when she encounters Shasta, but as she finds in her progressive adventures with him, she is also escaping a life stifled by her own smugness and snobbishness. At first, she can barely control the contempt she feels in having to travel and do business with one as lowly as Shasta. By the tale's end, and with Aslan's intervention, she realizes that character is everything and that the privileges of birth count for little.

Bree is everything Hwin is not: stubborn, prideful, and horribly superior in attitude and behavior. Hwin, by contrast, is tentative, shy, and self-effacing; she must gain in confidence what Bree must lose in arrogance. A typical scene shows the weary, faltering Hwin declaring with great courage:

> "I feel just like Bree that I *can't* go on. But when Horses have humans (with spurs and things) on their backs, aren't they often made to go on when they're feeling like this? and then they find they can. I m-mean—oughtn't we to be able to do more even, now that we're free."[22]

It is in Bree's nature to upstage her by suggesting, "I think, Ma'am . . . that I know a little more about campaigns and forced marches and what a horse can stand than you do." [23]

Bree must eventually begin the long journey to humility by hearing the words of the Hermit, the mysterious wise man they encounter: "You're not quite the great horse you had come to think. . . . But as long as you know you're nobody very special, you'll be a very decent sort of horse, on the whole."[24]

The Hermit lives on the southern border of Archenland, a calm and trusting soul who knows Aslan and is confident in his care. Embodying true humility, he is content to see the present and unable to view the future. He exhorts the fugitive Aravis and company that he has "never yet met any such thing as Luck," implying that what they have instead experienced is Providence—the tenderhearted but tough-minded foresight of a loving Creator, Aslan, who has directed their steps and brought them safely home. He declines to speculate on what everything may mean on their journey but assures the children that "if ever we need to know it, you may be sure that we shall."[25] His testimony resonates with Puddleglum's declaration in *The Silver Chair* that "there are no accidents."

When Bree finally encounters Aslan, he insults him by offering the uninformed view that "it would be quite absurd to suppose he is a *real* lion." He must finally admit that he "must be rather a fool" and must enter his homeland "in a rather subdued frame of mind," painfully recognizing "how little he knew about Narnian customs and what dreadful mistakes he might make."[26]

The quartet of heroes is eventually set a mission to accomplish apart from their own individual struggles— warning King Lune of Archenland of an impending attack from the south. In many ways, however, this is not a novel about facing external enemies but a tale of self-discovery. The antagonist is oneself, or, more specifically, one's exalted view of oneself—one's vanity.

Shasta's story complements that of Aravis, whose difficulties stem not from ignorance of who she is, but from knowing all too well—and taking excessive pride in it. In the story, the greatest example of this is Aravis's mistreatment of her stepmother's servant, and Aslan must address her meanness as symbolic of this deep pride. Consequently, when Aravis encounters Aslan, she realizes that it was he all along who was her unexpected teacher: "The scratches on your back, tear for tear, throb for throb, blood for blood, were equal to the stripes laid on the back of your stepmother's slave because of the drugged sleep you cast upon her. You needed to know what it felt like."[27]

Aravis learns fast enough to finally confess to Shasta, "There's something I've got to say at once. I'm sorry I've been such a pig. But I did change before I knew you were a Prince, honestly I did."[28]

Unlike Bree, whose arrogance must be stripped from him like Eustace's dragon skin, Hwin has a pure soul that gives her poise and purpose. When she comes before Aslan, she immediately recognizes her place before him:

"'Please,' she said, 'you're so beautiful. You may eat me if you like. I'd sooner be eaten by you than fed by anyone else.'"

In this surrender of self, she learns firsthand the tenderness of the one she is serving. "Dearest daughter, . . . I knew you would not be long in coming to me. Joy shall be yours."[29]

The Horse and His Boy forcefully dramatizes what Narnia scholar Colin Manlove explains as a meditation on freedom and responsibility where "each member of the party breaks out of his or her egoism or reserve and learns to relate, to share, and to help. And as they do, they make up a microcosmic Narnian state of free, democratic, equal, and varied individuals"[30] Only in Narnia, and only in Aslan's name, can four such diverse creatures conquer their fears, gain self-forgetfulness, and find their true home.

In a letter to a young lady in 1961, Lewis suggested that one meaning of the story was the calling and conversion of one outside the faith; that is, external to the traditions and history of Narnia.[31] Shasta surely undergoes a kind of conversion as a young man who has grown up not knowing his true father or his true identity. He is heathen in the sense that he does not know Aslan by name—but he emulates Aslan's character. As such, he foreshadows the compelling character of Emeth, who emerges in *The Last Battle* as both courageous and righteous, acting on the best motives even though he is not familiar with Aslan or the ethics of Narnia. Shasta, like Emeth, has learned to behave like a Narnian, even while still distant from his true home and lacking direct knowledge of his benefactor, Aslan.

The next chapter takes us from the realm of those whose greatest desire is to know Aslan to those whose greatest hope is to avoid him at all costs and to enslave or kill those who follow him.

CHAPTER 5

VILLAINY MEETS VICIOUSNESS:

Witches, Traitors, and Betrayers

*"This is no thaw," said the Dwarf, suddenly stopping. "This is spring. What are we to do?
Your winter has been destroyed, I tell you! This is Aslan's doing."*

"If either of you mention that name again," said the Witch, "he shall instantly be killed."[1]

THE LION, THE WITCH, AND THE WARDROBE

The study of evil, though theoretically possible, is inherently unrewarding, dangerous, and unquestionably tedious. We have all made entries in the catalog of wickedness both in prospect and deed, one way or another. In the Gospels, Jesus points out that having an adulterous heart is the same as committing the act and that hating someone is tantamount to murder. It is not as though studying evil helps us to better recognize and more capably avoid it. More likely, such knowledge will simply titillate us and expand our options for immoral behavior. If we look within ourselves, we already know evil's origins; and if we look outward to revelation, we also know its future. It has none. Evil is destined to be banished forever; death will soon lose its sting, and life will triumph. The real question is whose side we are on, and this is the essential question faced by Narnians and humans in the Chronicles.

In times of general order and basic happiness, with food in our stomachs and roofs over our heads, few of us think of evil, and fewer still of its mystery, of why it exists at all. Curiously, it is often when evil is impersonal and vague, yet pervasive—when a tsunami hits, when famine, plague, and ruin come—that we get serious about the whys and wherefores. World literatures of every tribe and tongue investigate this phenomenon. Why is there suffering, oppression, and heartache, and how can they be put right, in this world or the next?

The answers differ widely, but depersonified evil is not interesting in a narrative. In stories, evil needs a face.

No genre of fiction treats the problem of evil more systematically or graphically than the fairy tale, and the Chronicles are no exception. What is exceptional is that, in Narnia, the problem of the good is also addressed forthrightly and eloquently. We have already pointed out that depicting evil is less challenging than portraying good. All villainy in fiction basically works by cutting the evil person, the perpetrator, down to size. It is personalized in this or that villain, those thugs, or that warmonger. He, she, or they represent evil in their character, thoughts, and deeds. Close the book, and the evil goes away. But does it? The effects of evil can spill over and extend themselves in ways that are not immediately apparent. Unless the evil is met head on and the bad guys lose, evil escapes and spreads. The rumor that crime does pay, that one can get away with murder, must not be allowed to even start. Evil allowed to live beyond the reader's or listener's time within the story's landscape—evil that haunts or troubles one's waking life or dreams—this is the risk of contemplating evil too intently and too long.

Tales that do not merely depict evil but instead celebrate its reign without consequence are vile and demented. Stories that show what is good as debilitated or ineffectual and glorify villainy to the point of viciousness and vituperation deserve our scorn and refutation.

The greatest corrective, however, lies not in book burning and censorship but in writing and reading better, more compelling stories. It is the role of the author, and particularly of the Christian author, to explain and contain the flow of evil. This can occur only when evil is depicted as conquerable, when it is surmounted by Someone greater than the perpetrator, the evildoer's deeds, and evil itself.

How could any character or being be greater than evil? Even the greatest superheroes have their secret weaknesses—Achilles his heel, Superman his kryptonite. However, there is such a Hero, whose only vulnerability is that he loves us and cannot bear to see us descend into hell without a fight. As novelist Walker Percy puts it, "If you're a big enough fool to climb a tree and like a cat refuse to come down, then someone who loves you has to make as big a fool of himself to rescue you."[2]

Percy and I are speaking, of course, of the Christian story: the incarnation, crucifixion, resurrection, ascension, coronation, and victorious reign of the Son of God. This is also Narnia's story. Aslan is the Son of the great Emperor-beyond-the-Sea. He is not beyond good and evil; he meticulously follows his own rules, and no "dark side of the Force" maintains Narnia's equilibrium. Evil is not on one end of a continuum with good. The dark side has no chance. The drama in the story is that the dark side does not seem to be aware of this.

No, evil is evil and good is good. Good is always greater than evil and does not resemble it in any way. Evil is the counterfeit, the pathetic copy, good the everlasting original. The good, or those who are trying to be good, may stumble along the way or slip off the path. They may even permanently choose the wrong path and finally embrace a destiny of destruction. But with the grace and mercy of Aslan, King of Narnia (known by a different name in our world), even the wayward may be restored and the faltering find hope and strength to resist evil and return to the pursuit of the holy and the true.

C. S. Lewis was clear in expressing the value of the fairy tale in such an enterprise. We must not, he says, try to keep out of a child's mind "the knowledge that he is born into a world of death, violence, wounds, adventure, heroism and cowardice, good and evil." Rather, "let there be wicked kings and beheadings, battles and dungeons, giants and dragons, and let villains be soundly killed at the end of the book. Nothing will persuade me that this causes an ordinary child any kind or degree of fear beyond what it wants, and needs, to feel. For, of course, it wants to be a little frightened."[3]

Evil should frighten us, for it has the power to cause pain, loss, and eternal death, but evil need not overwhelm us. At its peak, there yet remains an answer, which is, simply, that good will triumph. This is as true in Narnia as it is in our world. Because we have traveled there, we already understand why Jadis, the White Witch, the Queen of the Underland, Uncle Andrew, and other fools and scoundrels populate Narnia. These criminals, rogues, and abusers parallel the ones in our world, and it is no good wishing them away in a candy-cane world of sweetness and light. Rather than be surprised by their appearance, we should be shocked if they did not exist in Narnia. As important as it is to know and trust that there is a world of wonder next door to ours, it is equally crucial for us to see that when villainy surfaces, it receives its just retribution, and evil is undone forever.

During the early 1940s, when war was on his mind and everyone else's, C. S. Lewis wrote the greatest studies of evil to be found in any century: *The Problem of Pain* (1941), *The Screwtape Letters* (1942), and *The Great Divorce* (1946). Each has its own influence in the Chronicles, but the demon Screwtape, who narrates advice to a junior devil in a series of letters on how to tempt a human ("patient") and wrestle him away from "the Enemy" (Christ), is most resonant. In imagining the wicked and prideful creatures who wreak havoc in Narnia, Lewis had good practice in using the reverse psychology needed to create Screwtape. Observing evil at its point of contact with good is most instructive, and that is where the battle is pitched in Narnia when evil queens, prideful traitors, and selfish betrayers meet Aslan and his friends.

Of the seven Narnia tales, the two stories that deal

most directly with the mystery of evil are *The Lion, the Witch, and the Wardrobe* and *The Magician's Nephew*, for in both, Aslan comes face to face with evil personified. *The Last Battle* also provides great insight into evil, and that book will have a whole chapter to itself, since it deals with evil's ultimate demise. It is useful to see through the eyes of evildoers, if only temporarily, for thereby we may see how distorted the good appears in the prism of their souls, how impure their thoughts become as they race to stay ahead of their impending doom, how myopic their worldview as their world disintegrates before them. Evil never looks so weak or impotent as when it is juxtaposed with what is true and righteous. Aslan's righteous strength, his unsurpassed knowledge, and his supreme reign guarantee that the viciousness of villains will be vanquished forever—in Narnia and everywhere else.

JADIS, QUEEN OF NARNIA, IN *THE MAGICIAN'S NEPHEW* AND THE WHITE WITCH IN *THE LION, THE WITCH, AND THE WARDROBE*

We meet the White Witch first in *The Lion, the Witch, and the Wardrobe* as she turns disobedient creatures to stone, keeps Narnia under a perpetual winter storm warning, and rewards traitors—like Edmund—who cooperate with her. With the White Witch, it is "always winter and never Christmas," an apt picture of her soul.[4] Even the name Aslan is loathsome to her, as our

122

epigraph illustrates. Her confrontations with Aslan—including her backstory as Jadis, Queen of Narnia, told in *The Magician's Nephew*—comprise the most revealing episodes about the triumph of good over the emptiness of evil in the Chronicles. When evil tries to match wits with good, its ignorance is transparent, its insignificance revealed.

When Lewis created the Chronicles of Narnia, he did not have to contend much with the category of "the good witch" prominent in modern culture, particularly in the genre of children's fantasy. (This innovation appears to get its impetus from Glinda the Good Witch in *The Wizard of Oz*.) Lewis's characterization of the White Witch jars the literary imagination, because the color white is usually associated with purity. At one time, a witch or sorcerer was evil by definition. In inventing bad creatures, Lewis relied to a large degree on stock characters. In other words, he relied on characters already established in his readers' minds as exemplifying evil, without elaborate exposition and description. Fairy tales are full of such stock characters, as are the writings of Shakespeare.

A witch is up to no good, and that's that. Her particular treachery may be singularly perverse and disastrous, but her character need not be explained or justified—her outside betrays her inside. Evil is monotonous, unimaginative, predictable, flat, and colorless. Its essence is pride, its product utter selfishness. By contrast, good is diverse, multihued, fascinating, and enduring. There are many ways to be good, because goodness is infinite in its manifestations. There is but one way to be evil: to "be oneself" to the nth degree without regard for how self-exaltation affects or corrodes the lives around us.

The White Witch is pretentiously stately, easily bored, and curious only when the answer to a question increases her power or strengthens her authority. Her perception and memory are selective; she is susceptible to self-deception and superior knowledge, even when uttered by a child or a teenager. When she first encounters Edmund, she mistakes him for "a great overgrown dwarf that has cut off its beard."[5] Having not seen a human being since she and Uncle Andrew encountered Digory, Polly, Frank, and Helen at the creation of Narnia, the White Witch doesn't immediately recognize Edmund as a Son of Adam. As soon as she does, she offers him a bribe, since her only means of dealing with her subjects is manipulation or outright intimidation. Edmund succumbs to Turkish Delight, a childish but powerful symbol of the ease with which the faint-hearted can be duped into surrendering their allegiance to an object or person unworthy of them. Soon, however, Edmund's envy and jealousy toward his siblings are all the White Witch needs to drive his treachery; he is soon consumed with dreams of being a prince and reigning in Narnia. Under her dominion, Edmund seems not to notice how cold, dreary, and menacing eternal winter can be. Such is the power of evil over our imaginations.

In this case, the White Witch has picked on someone her own size. Adding Edmund to her corps of nasty informants is no particular achievement. But what does evil see when it looks at Someone superior in integrity, veracity, and authority? When the Witch is confronted with the word and presence of Aslan, she sees only an enemy, an impediment to her total command that she completely underestimates, regarding him as a fool for opposing her. The bully in her cannot conceive of a greater good—indeed, no conception of "good" at all, for that requires a dethroning of self, of which she is incapable. In the climax of *The Lion, the Witch, and the Wardrobe*, she arranges a rendezvous with Aslan, the rightful King and heir to all things, and finds herself uncomfortable next to a true Sovereign who voluntarily lays down his life for another. She cannot comprehend him. She has never met someone capable of saying, as did missionary Jim Elliot, "He is no fool who gives what he cannot keep to gain what he cannot lose."[6]

The selfish and the egotistical know only self-aggrandizement: "Any for you means less for me, so you shall have none at all." The Witch is an equal-opportunity assassin. She would reign for the sake of reigning, not because it serves her kingdom or its citizens. She is morally blind, incapable of seeing from another's point of view. The White Witch is not completely lawless, but she believes herself to be above the law. In their repartee over Edmund's fate, Aslan and the White Witch reveal their respective value systems:

"Well," said Aslan, "his offense was not against you."

"Have you forgotten the Deep Magic?" asked the Witch.

"Let us say I have forgotten it," answered Aslan gravely. "Tell us of this Deep Magic."[7]

The White Witch knows the law, the Deep Magic from the dawn of time. She is "by the book" and can "quote Scripture like the devil," since she is descended from the father of lies. But her knowledge of the Deep Magic is not the same thing as being willing to obey it; she is only willing to enforce it as the Emperor's executioner, and then only if it is to her perceived advantage.

"Tell you? . . . Tell you what is written in letters deep as a spear is long on the trunk of the World Ash Tree? Tell you what is engraved on the scepter of the Emperor-beyond-the-Sea? You at least know the magic which the Emperor put into Narnia at the very beginning. You know that every traitor belongs to me as my lawful prey and that for every treachery I have a right to kill. . . . And so . . . that Human creature is mine. His life forfeit to me. His blood is my property."[8]

The Deep Magic for her, like everything else in her reign, is just something that can be forged into a weapon against Narnians; her black magic can subdue, subjugate, and suppress; and she can turn creatures into stone.

She already has a heart of stone, so she is merely making others over into her image. But it appears that some of Aslan's followers might take up arms against her.

"'Fool,' said the Witch with a savage smile that was almost a snarl, 'do you really think your master can rob me of my rights by mere force? He knows the Deep Magic better than that. He knows that unless I have blood as the Law says, all Narnia will be overturned and perish in fire and water.'"[9]

Aslan acknowledges that this is, in fact, the essence of the Deep Magic; it was designed to discourage and punish betrayers: "It is very true, . . . I do not deny it."

Susan is immediately horrified with this verdict, and pleads, "Oh Aslan! . . . Can't we—I mean, you won't, will you? Can't we do something about the Deep Magic? Isn't there something you can work against it?"

Such a sentiment, though understandable in the passion of the moment, is ill-thought and reflects Susan's naïveté and limited judgment. Aslan's reply is swift and decisive: "Work against the Emperor's magic?"[10]

Such a response is unthinkable—and Susan does not realize what she is asking. The law that preserves Narnia's fragile civility and hope for freedom cannot be undermined and perverted to save a confessed traitor. It would put them on a level with the surly rabble who stood before the cross and called upon Christ to come down from the cross and save himself.

This would not rescue Edmund, and it would put

the whole of Narnia in jeopardy. Worst of all, it would betray Aslan's Father. The wise and mighty Aslan has, however, a better plan that will honor his Father and save Narnia. When Aslan proposes to ransom Edmund's life with his own, the White Witch completely misunderstands where this terrible calamity is headed:

> "And now, who has won? Fool, did you think that by all this you would save the human traitor? Now I will kill you instead of him as our pact was and so the Deep Magic will be appeased. But when you are dead what will prevent me from killing him as well? And who will take him out of my hand *then?* Understand that you have given me Narnia for ever, you have lost your own life, and you have not saved his. In that knowledge, despair and die."[11]

The Witch has only a few fragments, not the complete picture. She has memorized the part of the law that benefits her—the part that reflects the consequences of letting a traitor live, unpunished. She has already destroyed the world of Charn, and she would settle for destroying Narnia, as prophesied, if she could not execute Edmund or Aslan. How ignorant she is; how incredible a proposition it is to her that anyone, much less Aslan, should lay down his life for another!

She never sees it coming. There is a deeper magic from before the dawn of time; as Aslan patiently tells

Lucy and Susan after his triumphant resurrection to life:

> "Though the Witch knew the Deep Magic, there is a magic deeper still which she did not know. Her knowledge goes back only to the dawn of Time. But if she could have looked a little further back, into the stillness and the darkness before Time dawned, she would have read there a different incantation. She would have known that when a willing victim who had committed no treachery was killed in a traitor's stead, the Table would crack and Death itself would start working backward."[12]

The Deeper Magic restores life and dispenses justice.

Aslan takes pains to explain why the White Witch failed even to be a resourceful villainess. Her knowledge went back only to the dawn of time; it was temporal, partial, and idiosyncratic, and it did not derive from outside Narnia. She had settled for what can be known "under the sun" and had not hungered and thirsted for anything more. This is characteristic of evil antagonists in many fantasy tales in which willful ignorance, mistaken for knowledge, kills its possessor.

When Tolkien refers to the death and resurrection of Christ as a *eucatastrophe* (a "good catastrophe," or "happy tragedy," from the Greek *eu-*, which means "good") in his masterful essay, "On Fairy Stories," he is drawing attention to a similarly fatal flaw for villainy: Evil is shortsighted. Because evildoers can see only what is immediately useful to gaining or maintaining power, their judgment is clouded and their single-minded egotism prevents them from understanding the ramifications of their actions. A good man or woman can outwit or outlive the deeds of evildoers because he or she recognizes that mere self-survival is a less-than-ultimate good. In Tolkien's example, the apparently colossal tragedy of the death of God's Son turns out to be the very means by which God destroys Satan's power. It is thus the world's greatest practical joke. In his death and resurrection, the Son proves his superiority and silences the father of lies forever. In Genesis 3:15, the serpent thinks he is killing God's servant ("ye shall bruise his heel"), but instead, he initiates his own destruction ("but he shall crush your head"). So, too, does the White Witch.

As we discover in *The Magician's Nephew*, there is much that Jadis has never understood, especially about magic. There is an important distinction to be drawn in Narnia between two kinds of magic. The magic that emanates from Aslan is not deception or sleight of hand but true, miraculous power. Though it is called magic as a concession to the humans who visit, it is actually a "Deeper Magic" that is set in the very fabric of the universe in which Narnia and our world exist. It is based upon real and eternal principles that transcend time, also known as obedient goodness. This is the magic that creates out of nothing, resurrects the dead, empowers the valiant to be faithful in battle, reverses the spells of villains and evildoers, and ensures that good triumphs over evil. It belongs to Aslan by virtue of his kingly role and because he alone is good. Those who belong to Narnia follow Aslan and partake of this goodness by doing what Aslan does; yet in the end, only Aslan's freely bestowed love, mercy, and grace preserve their lives.

The other kind of magic is built upon trickery and guile; it is dark magic used to manipulate nature and to confuse conscious and conscientious creatures. Jadis's use of the Deplorable Word to destroy Charn represents mad, selfish, evil power at its worst. C. S. Lewis scholar Alice Cook has pointed out that Lewis defines magic as "an attempt to subdue reality to the wishes of men" and suggests that in his work characters who "long for power without paying its price" become partners in the magician's bargain to "give up the soul [and] get power in return."[13] This is an apt description of Jadis, yet when Digory first meets her, he thinks of her as beautiful and alluring ("She's wonderfully brave. And strong. She's what I call a Queen!")—a reaction Polly does not share, to say the least.[14] He soon sees that Jadis's supposed beauty is not even skin deep, but is itself a kind of spell. Her charm begins to fade when she matter-of-factly confesses to the murder of her sister and all the former inhabitants of Charn.

"Look well on that which no eyes will ever see again. . . . Such was Charn, that great city, the city of the King of Kings, the wonder of the world, perhaps of all worlds. . . . It is silent now. But I have stood here when the whole air was full of the noises of Charn." . . . All in one moment one woman blotted it out for ever.[15]

Her coldness and bravado astound Digory and anger Polly, but her ego is boundless:

"I," said the Queen. "I, Jadis, the last Queen, but the Queen of the world . . . spoke the Deplorable Word. A moment later I was the only living thing beneath the sun."[16]

Her freewheeling admission of genocide is breathtaking; her preference to be alone rather than share her world with others conveys, undeniably and monstrously, the heart of darkness, the epitome of evil. She, of course, has her rationale: *noblesse oblige*.

"I had forgotten that you are only a common boy. How should you understand reasons of State? You must learn, child, that what would be wrong for you or for any of the common people is not wrong in a great Queen such as I. The weight of the world is on our shoulders. We must be freed from all rules. Ours is a high and lonely destiny."[17]

Jadis's "Deplorable Word" is spoken in stark contrast to the Song of Aslan, which creates life, beauty, color, shape, form, and, most of all, communion. Jadis has no wish to know another person, to share intimately in their dreams, hopes, or aspirations. She is barely a person, only an entity with a name, who is slowly and inevitably sinking down into herself and will soon be next to nothing, mere existence, a zero with no dimensions. This is, as Lewis has George Macdonald explain in *The Great Divorce*, the essence of those whose citizenship is in hell:

> "And yet all loneliness, angers, hatreds, envies, and itchings that [Hell] contains, if rolled into one single experience and put into the scale against the least moment of the joy that is felt by the least in Heaven, would have no weight that could be registered at all. Bad cannot succeed even in being bad as truly as good is good. If all Hell's miseries together entered the consciousness of yon wee yellow bird on the bough there, they would be swallowed up without trace, as if one drop of ink had been dropped into that Great Ocean to which your terrestrial Pacific itself is only a molecule."[18]

Jadis can destroy, but only Aslan can create out of nothing. Even she recognizes the difference, however reluctantly, as she stands a safe distance away from Narnia's creation: "This is not Charn," came the Witch's voice. "This is an empty world. This is Nothing."[19]

On the canvas before them, Aslan was painting with light:

> In the darkness something was happening at last. A voice had begun to sing. It was very far away and Digory found it hard to decide from what direction it was coming.[20]

Jadis, however, has no ear for such a tune:

> Ever since the song began she had felt that this whole world was filled with a Magic different from hers, and stronger. She hated it. She would have smashed that whole world, or all worlds, to pieces, if it would only stop the singing.[21]

The majesty of Aslan is too much for her to bear:

> It was a Lion. Huge, shaggy, and bright, it stood facing the risen sun. Its mouth was wide open in song and it was about three hundred yards away.
>
> "This is a terrible world," said the Witch. "We must fly at once. Prepare the Magic."[22]

The dark magic enjoined here by Jadis, employed by the Queen of the Underland in *The Silver Chair*, sought by Nikabrik in *Prince Caspian*, and pitifully attempted by Uncle Andrew, is derived from sheer greed and ruthless power—the desire to rule over creation through manip-

NOT A TAME LION

ulation and deceit. Creativity, light, beauty, truth, justice, selflessness—through the eyes of the wicked these are indeed "terrible," reminding them even in their scarred remnant of a conscience that Aslan's world is not safe, but good, and that the hardhearted cannot abide that goodness for long. It shames and exposes, convicts, and demands repentance and restitution. Such responses require humble confession—impossible for those who refuse redemption. As Lewis puts it in *The Problem of Pain*, "I willingly believe that the damned are, in one sense, successful, rebels to the end; that the doors of hell are locked on the inside."[23]

This is a useful diagnosis of the inscrutably treacherous Jadis, who evolves into the implacable, scheming White Witch of *The Lion, the Witch, and the Wardrobe*. Aslan knows her well, of course, for he has created all things, even her. The exact source of her evil character is mysterious, but as with all Lewis's villains, the central core of her motivation is pride and arrogance, both of which Jadis has in abundance. Aslan assures Digory and Polly that the effects of Jadis's having eaten the same apple that brings life to Digory's dying mother will not be so salutary for Jadis.

Things always work according to their nature. Jadis has won her heart's desire for unwearying strength and endless days like a goddess. But with her evil heart, length of days is only length of misery, and already she begins to know it. All get what they want, but they do not always like it. Her fate is that of all who desire to be immortally "themselves," like those in Lewis's *The Problem of Pain:*

> In the long run the answer to all those who object to the doctrine of hell is itself a question: "What are you asking God to do?" To wipe out their past sins and, at all costs, to give them a fresh start, smoothing every difficulty and offering every miraculous help? But He has done so, on Calvary. To forgive them? They will not be forgiven. To leave them alone? Alas, I am afraid that is what He does.[24]

UNCLE ANDREW IN
THE MAGICIAN'S NEPHEW

Uncle Andrew is a foolish, self-righteous, vain individual who, despite his age, is not a grown-up. Lewis deploys his character as a vivid reminder that age alone is no guarantee of wisdom or good judgment. Embodied in Uncle Andrew's choices in *The Magician's Nephew* is a thirst for illegal authority and unwarranted power, and the consequences of his trickery and misuse of the rings are portrayed in graphic detail. Lewis makes it clear that Uncle Andrew is dangerous; he pursues unlawful magic, and he is a vivisectionist who uses animals for experiments and treats them cruelly for his own vile purposes. Cruelty to animals was a trait Lewis could not abide, and he wrote about this in several essays and editorials.

Uncle Andrew's cowardly actions indirectly lead to Digory's immature and foolish awakening of the evil Jadis. Uncle Andrew also threatens life in his own world by making it possible for Jadis to spread her treachery to the streets of London. That her power does not work in London is a grace from Aslan. Uncle Andrew is accustomed to nefarious deeds. The rings that permit his travel to other worlds, as well as his vanity and thirst for unsavory power over others, are an inheritance from his infernal godmother, Mrs. Lefay—an echo of the Arthurian tradition wherein Arthur's half-sister Morgan Lefay contributes to the destruction of Camelot. Uncle Andrew's weak character and lust for power make him easy prey for Jadis, who makes him her pawn in much the way that the White Witch uses Edmund in *The Lion, the Witch, and the Wardrobe.*

Unlike the noble quests upon which many Narnian characters embark after a call from Aslan, Uncle Andrew's "experiment" is purely selfish and cowardly. There is a telling moment when the full force of Uncle Andrew's gross immaturity and callous disregard for others is dramatically evident to Digory:

> "Oh, I see. You mean that little boys ought to keep their promises. Very true. Most right and proper, I'm sure, and I'm very glad you have been taught to do it. But of course you must understand that rules of that sort, however excellent they may be for little

boys—and servants—and women—and even people in general, can't possibly be expected to apply to profound students and great thinkers and sages. No, Digory. Men like me who possess hidden wisdom are freed from common rules just as we are cut off from common pleasures. Ours, my boy, is a high and lonely destiny."[25]

"Hidden wisdom" is the code word that exposes Uncle Andrew's prideful ignorance and lack of valor; it is akin to Jadis's haughty understanding of "deep magic." This phrasing tips Digory off to his uncle's basic dishonesty, and Jadis reveals her corruption by repeating similar phrases when he and Polly later meet her. Digory knows pretentious nonsense when he hears it.

As he said this he sighed and looked so grave and no-ble and mysterious that for a second Digory really thought he was saying something rather fine. . . . All at once he saw through Uncle Andrew's grand words. All it means, he said to himself, is that he thinks he can do anything he likes to get anything he wants.[26]

Digory is destined to be Lord Digory, Professor Kirke, a noble hero of Narnia, and a tested and tried man of integrity. His long-suffering pursuit of righteousness gives him the strength to resist Uncle Andrew's lies and perversity and follow his heart, which compels him to rescue Polly and save his mother.

Aslan sees the courage in both Digory and Polly, and reveals that he has all along been preparing them for more adventure, not only in Narnia, but on both sides of the Wood:

> "It is not certain that some wicked one of your race will not find out a secret as evil as the Deplorable Word and use it to destroy all living things. And soon, very soon, before you are an old man and an old woman, great nations in your world will be ruled by tyrants who care no more for joy and justice and mercy than the Empress Jadis. Let your world beware. That is the warning. Now for the command. As soon as you can, take from this uncle of yours his magic Rings and bury them so that no one can use them again."[27]

The wicked and the selfish live fearfully in desperation and loneliness. The valorous and the intrepid are prepared by their vision to serve Aslan in this world and in the world beyond.

THE QUEEN OF THE UNDERLAND IN *THE SILVER CHAIR*

Like other evil characters in Narnia, this Witch Queen also attempts to bypass the natural order of Narnia through lies and black magic. Her strategy is relentless attack on her subjects' sense of reality, as she impugns both their reason and their imagination. She powerfully conveys falsehood and spreads propaganda against the very idea of an Overland, a sunny kingdom belonging to Aslan.

Puddleglum, Eustace, and Jill finally find the bound Prince Rilian. For a brief period each day he is sane, but they cannot release him until they overcome the lies that they have been told as to who he is and what will happen if he is freed from the Silver Chair. At last, he speaks the final sign: "I adjure you to set me free. By all fears and all loves, by the bright skies of Overland, by the great Lion, by Aslan himself, I charge you."[28]

By Aslan's name, they now know the truth, but that truth is under attack once they come into the Queen's lair. Through ridicule and scorn, she inveighs against their belief: "Narnia? . . . Narnia? . . . There is no land called Narnia."[29]

As Jill begins to drift into unbelief, she finds herself saying, "No, I suppose that other world must be all a dream."

The Queen, sensing Jill's vulnerability, seizes the moment: "Yes. It *is* all a dream. . . . There never was such a world."[30]

In what she thinks will be her final blow, the Queen rails against Aslan's existence, using reductionist thinking to explain everything away. She uses apparent logic against their mere "make-believe":

> "You have seen lamps, and so you imagined a bigger and better lamp and called it the *sun*. You've seen cats, and now you want a bigger and better cat, and it's to be called a *lion*. Well, 'tis a pretty make-believe, though, to say truth, it would suit you all better if you were younger. And look how you can put nothing into your make-believe world without copying it from the real world, this world of mine, which is the only world. . . . Put away these childish tricks. I have work for you all in the real world. There is no Narnia, no Overworld, no sky, no sun, no Aslan."[31]

The Queen's ploy fails when her serpentine identity is revealed in her sudden wrath against Puddleglum's masterful refutation. The Queen's disenchantments fail, but only because the children's resolve is strengthened by the power of Aslan's gifts of reason and imagination, tethered to faith; these dispel falsehood and reaffirm the truth stored in their heart of hearts. The Marsh-wiggle exercises both reason and imagination, and he alone remains steadfast in his trust that Aslan "knew already all things that would come" and would be true to his word.[32]

    The Queen's tactics resemble the advice that senior devil Screwtape offers to Wormwood in *The Screwtape*

Letters, as he undermines the earth dwellers' faith in their true homeland:

> "Prosperity knits a man to the World. He feels that he is 'finding his place in it,' while really it is finding its place in him. His increasing reputation, his widening circle of acquaintances, his sense of importance, the growing pressure of absorbing and agreeable work, build up in him a sense of being really at home in earth which is just what we want. . . . The truth is that the Enemy, having oddly destined these mere animals to life in His own eternal world, has guarded them pretty effectively from the danger of feeling at home anywhere else. That is why we must often wish long life to our patients; seventy years is not a day too much for the difficult task of unraveling their souls from Heaven and building up a firm attachment to the earth. . . . So inveterate is their appetite for Heaven that our best method, at this stage, of attaching them to earth is to make them believe that earth can be turned into Heaven at some future date by politics or eugenics or 'science' or psychology or what not."[33]

The climax of *The Silver Chair* teaches a lesson of the other Narnia tales in a slightly different way. Aslan is not a tame lion, but neither are those who follow him tame. In this story, the defeat of evil and the restoration of rightful rule emerge from faithful behavior and attention paid to Aslan's words, rather than from Aslan's direct intervention.

Our life in Narnia, our future in heaven—these are not dreams but reality. In his world and in ours, obedience and fidelity to the truth are needed to win the day. We need not listen to the Queen or to Screwtape. Heaven is our home, and earth our temporary way station.

NIKABRIK IN *PRINCE CASPIAN*

Of all the sad stories of bewitched and bewildered creatures in Narnia who become captive to evil, none is more mournful than the tale of Nikabrik. This unbelieving dwarf, incapable of overcoming his profound distrust of the old stories, epitomizes a different aspect of evil's lure and devastation. Nikabrik—like the band of self-seeking dwarfs we will observe in chapter 6—is world weary and skeptical. When asked if he believes in Aslan, he shrugs that he will believe in "anyone or anything" who will throw off the yoke of King Miraz's oppression: "Anyone or anything, Aslan or the White Witch, do you understand?" Though rebuked by the more cultured and respectful Trufflehunter, Nikabrik still harbors his doubts and nurtures his cynicism.

As events progress, the impatient and unschooled Nikabrik, rejecting out of hand the promise of help from ancient prophecies or the mobilization of Caspian's friends, instead puts his trust in his companions, a hag and a werewolf, and plans to call upon the dark magic of the long dead White Witch:

> "All said and done," he muttered, "none of us knows the truth about the ancient days in Narnia. . . . Aslan and the Kings go together. Either Aslan is dead, or he is not on our side. Or else something stronger than himself keeps him back. And if he did come—how do we know he'd be our friend? . . . Anyway, he was in Narnia only once that I ever heard of, and he didn't stay long. You may drop Aslan out of the reckoning. I was thinking of someone else."[34]

This is the voice of despair and alienation masquerading as the voice of reason. So distant is he from Narnia's traditions—its history, its promise, and its relationship to its Creator and King, Aslan—that Nikabrik can seriously contemplate "a power so much greater than Aslan's," which he believes has "held Narnia spellbound for years and years, if the stories are true."[35] Falsehood has become truth, black has become white, destruction has become destiny.

This is Lewis's cautionary tale to any civilization inebriated by self-importance and the supposed ability to thrive without historical perspective or relationship with God. This is chronological snobbery gone wild, a disposition to disbelieve the old stories and to substitute a contrary meaning for the original. In the end, Nikabrik confesses:

> "Yes. . . . I mean the Witch. . . . We want power: and we want a power that will be on our side. As for power, do not the stories say that the Witch defeated Aslan, and bound him, and killed him on that very stone which is over there, just beyond the light?"[36]

When the badger and others counter his virulent, militant unbelief, Nikabrik bellows:

> "Yes, they *say*, . . . but you'll notice that we hear precious little about anything he did afterwards. He just fades out of the story. How do you explain that, if he really came to life? Isn't it much more likely that he didn't, and that the stories say nothing more about him because there was nothing more to say? . . . They say [the White Witch] ruled for a hundred years: a hundred years of winter. There's power, if you like. There's something practical."[37]

The Hag adds, "Who ever heard of a witch that really died? You can always get them back."[38]

To Nikabrik, this witch never dies, and her power to sustain winter for a hundred years is more impressive than the return of the rightful King. Nikabrik will rally the treasonous ne'er-do-wells to revive her through necromancy, and this will be the foundation of the new society Nikabrik envisions for himself and his fellow dwarfs and outcasts. But this cannot happen as long as there are those who know and practice the truth.

The final, trustworthy story of Narnia is written by the followers of Aslan. That grand narrative must be told and retold with accurate attention to detail in the way that Dr. Cornelius passed it on to Prince Caspian. It must be preserved, and most importantly, it must be enacted, for it is our true story; it both retells and fore-tells our destiny. To divorce oneself from this history, from the true character of Aslan and the real adventures of his loyal subjects, is to sentence oneself to disen-chantment, self-doubt, and despair. In our times, more passive but nonetheless effective weapons of evil have arisen, an arsenal that resides in every culture that jetti-sons its historical roots and reinvents itself at will. These include the big lie, the doctored report, the dis-torted original, the reversed interpretation, the delib-erately forgotten premise, and, most deviously, the cultivation of historical distrust. Such distrust fosters the attitude that if history can't be changed, one should ignore it or make up one's own.

Puddleglum, Caspian, Rilian, Tirian, Jewel, and many other Narnian heroes all testify to the need to re-sist these tactics as actively as we would resist sheer vi-olence and physical intimidation. These vicious and callous acts begin in the unredeemed reason and imagination, in the deceit and cunning of those who would mock our view of Aslan's country, and undermine the promise of our citizenship there. Vigilance against this vile manipulation is the message of *The Last Battle*, to which we now turn.

CHAPTER 6

VINDICATION AND VALEDICTION:
Last Battles, Last Words

*"Yes, and I did hope," said Jill, "that it might go on forever. I knew our world couldn't.
I did think Narnia might."*

"I saw it begin," said the Lord Digory. "I did not think I would live to see it die."

*"Sirs," said Tirian, "the ladies do well to weep. See, I do so myself. I have seen
my mother's death. What world but Narnia have I ever known? It were no virtue,
but great discourtesy, if we did not mourn."*[1]

THE LAST BATTLE

SUGGESTED READING FOR THIS CHAPTER:

Because this chapter focuses on most of *The Last Battle*,
you may want to reread the entire volume.

The opening pages of *The Last Battle* announce that we are in the last days of Narnia. This is an unwelcome greeting to readers who have been on the journey this long and now seek to extend their adventures among old and new Narnian friends. We want Narnia to go on forever. Nobody ever wants a good story to end, and a great story that bolsters our loyalty and confidence and rewards our faith is especially hard to relinquish.

But it is fitting for the end to come, because vindication comes only in the end, with valediction. Aslan's rewards for what we have done in his name are the understanding of what our lives have meant and the validation of who we have become. We long to hear "Well done, thou good and faithful servant" from our Master. This is simultaneously a benediction (a "good word," or blessing) and a valediction (a leave-taking and commission). An ending such as this, like the valedictory speech at a high school graduation, brings the graduates' years of schooling to a reflective close while also opening their future to them. With "last words" we revisit, remember, and register the meaning of the whole; we recount the beginning and the end—and look beyond both to our continuing destiny. The seven stories of Narnia reveal the meanings of the lives contained within their pages and the ways in which they are consequential to our own journeys.

Last things preoccupy us. We wonder about the last chapter, the final score, and how the movie ends. There is satisfaction in learning what comes next, of course; but there is also unique satisfaction in knowing what is finished, with loose ends tied up and closure achieved, tensions resolved. There is glory in completion. On the cross, Jesus declared to the Father, "It is finished," meaning, among many things, that our redemption through his substitutionary death for us was accomplished. There is great joy in knowing that history is going somewhere; it will come to a fitting conclusion in which justice will be realized under an administration of grace and mercy. New Testament Scripture attests to the desire God has "for the maturity of the times and the climax of the ages to unify all things and head them up and consummate them in Christ, [both] things in heaven and things on the earth" (Ephesians 1:10, AMP).

The "nextness" of our lives can overwhelm us—there is always another item on our cascading to-do list. We need to know we have run the course, finished the race, and fulfilled our destinies. What if we lived in a world in which nothing ever finally and completely came to a close? The truth is that we, "upon whom the end of the ages has come," *do* live in such a world. Paul reminds us that, in this cosmos, our earnest desire is not for endless time or perpetual postponement of the finish line, but consummation:

Yet what we suffer now is nothing compared to the glory he will reveal to us later. For all creation is waiting eagerly for that future day when God will reveal who his children really are. Against its will, all creation was subjected to God's curse. But with eager hope, the creation looks forward to the day when it will join God's children in glorious freedom from death and decay. For we know that all creation has been groaning as in the pains of childbirth right up to the present time. And we believers also groan, even though we have the Holy Spirit within us as a foretaste of future glory, for we long for our bodies to be released from sin and suffering. We, too, wait with eager hope for the day when God will give us our full rights as his adopted children, including the new bodies he has promised us. We were given this hope when we were saved. (If we already have something, we don't need to hope for it. But if we look forward to something we don't yet have, we must wait patiently and confidently.) ROMANS 8:18-25, NLT

"All creation is waiting eagerly for that future day." The day we long for is the last day, the unknown date whereupon all shall be revealed, our journey ended, and every account closed. We may know, here and there, the worth and satisfaction of a job well done, but we do not know completeness. God alone knows this, because he is outside time. Aslan knows this in his existence between worlds—as we also exist, if we could only realize it.

We struggle to come to grips with our mortality. In our still future immortality, the unimaginably rich quality of life and the absence of time to mark our progress will shock and reframe our identities. Our temporal life has been wrapped up in bodies that will wear out, but we will emerge as the eternal God-imaged Son or Daughter whose identity we have known only in fragments through our dreams and imagination. We are made for another world that cannot begin until the present one ends. Those who look to it for vindication and salvation in the name of Aslan, or of Christ, will find it a day for joy, celebration, and consummation. For others, who have refused knowledge of "the Deeper Magic before the dawn of time," it will be a day of humiliation in which "every knee shall bow and every tongue confess" to the true King (Romans 14:11). For them, it will not be a day of rejoicing, but of reckoning.

In their breadth and depth, the Narnia tales provide an uncommon vista of wholeness and symmetry, of Alpha and Omega, that is accessible to both younger and older readers. The tales allow us glimpses of the creation and maintenance of a universe through the entry of a loving Author into his own story. Aslan participates in the trials of his finite creatures in a time-space world that must yield to immortality through final judgment and consummation. Lewis provides a nonfictional exposition of this phenomenon in *Mere Christianity:*

I wonder whether people who ask God to interfere openly and directly in our world quite realise what it will be like when He does. When that happens, it is the end of the world. When the author walks on to the stage the play is over. God is going to invade, all right: but what is the good of saying you are on His side then, when you see the whole natural universe melting away like a dream and something else—something it never entered your head to conceive—comes crashing in; something so beautiful to some of us and so terrible to others that none of us will have any choice left? For this time it will be God without disguise; something so overwhelming that it will strike either irresistible love or irresistible horror into every creature. It will be too late then to choose your side. There is no use saying you choose to lie down when it has become impossible to stand up. That will not be the time for choosing: it will be the time when we discover which side we really have chosen, whether we realized it before or not. Now, today, this moment, is our chance to choose the right side. God is holding back to give us that chance. It will not last for ever. We must take it or leave it.[2]

In many ways, *The Last Battle* is one colossally integrated metaphor for the release and the relief of consummation. The image of the Shadow-Lands from the title of the last chapter gives us one point of entry. As referenced in *The Last Battle*, the Shadow-Lands refer to our world as a penultimate world—not the world of reality and light that is to come, nor the world as it should be or once was before the Fall, but this world as a vale of tears and shadows. For Lewis, the term echoed Plato's allegorical cave. It also suggests the pilgrims of the book of Hebrews, who lived in the shadow of the world that the Son of God came to reveal and whose "better country" they would not find here, but only hereafter. As the *Shadowlands* movie script says, "Our real life has not yet begun." The stories of this world fade into the sunset, and the enduring stories of eternity are yet to be written.

Perhaps this is the place to mention that other Narnia tales may be published by new authors to celebrate and extend Lewis's legacy. The idea is that there are yet stories to be told, more to be known about each character, and other relationships and landscapes to be explored. No doubt this is true, at least in our hearts. But no writer can exhaustively expand and infinitely arrange the characters, events, and dynamics of his literary universe. There is always something left to be said, and more to dream about. Even in the Gospels, the apostle John says, "Jesus did many other miraculous signs in the presence of his disciples, which are not recorded in this book. But these are written that you may believe that Jesus is the Christ, the Son of God, and that by believing you may have life in his name. . . . Jesus did many other things as well. If every one of them were written down, I suppose that even the whole world would not have room for the books that would be written" (John 20:30-31; 21:25).

Oh, to have those books, too, we say. But isn't it the point that we have what we need for belief in Jesus as the Christ? What God has granted us is sufficient.

There is something vaguely unseemly about a new set of Narnia tales, except, of course, for the ones that continue to tantalize us in our heads. The new tales will be backfill. What really happened to Susan? How did Puddleglum get to be so, er, glum? Over what other countries does Aslan reign? Telling these stories will interrupt, distract, and marginalize the seven Chronicles we have. This is a judgment about propriety, courtesy, and the ability to let an author's work stand on its own without the "help" of enterprising marketers and editors, whatever their credentials.

The prospect of new Narnia tales raises the issue of who Narnia belongs to. The answer is that Narnia belongs to Aslan, and no plot or theme that leaves him out or marginalizes him can be truly Narnian. For when we meet Aslan and good King Tirian in the seventh and last Chronicle, Narnia is once again in dire straits, chiefly because its citizens have forgotten what it means to be Narnian, a direct result of having forgotten who Aslan is.

NOT A TAME LION REVISITED

By the era depicted in *The Last Battle*, Mr. Beaver's earlier characterization of Aslan as an Untame Lion has become a byword—a slogan that is very nearly a lament. This designation of Aslan is voiced eight times, first in perplexity by Tirian and Jewel, and later by the evil Shift, who uses it as a cruel chant to silence and subjugate the talking beasts of Narnia. A group of dwarfs liberated from slavery but resistant and headstrong in their adamant unbelief later recite the phrase to deride those who follow Aslan. We wonder how Aslan's regal reputation could have fallen into vulgar speech.

King Tirian and his faithful unicorn friend, Jewel, though hoping it is true that Aslan has returned, dispute the reports because they have not detected it in the stars. Aslan sometimes uses the stars to foretell his coming, and Tirian and Jewel believe that if he were present, "all the gracious stars would be assembled in his honour." Still, they must allow for the fact that Aslan rules the stars and not the other way around.

"I wonder," said Jewel, "whether Aslan might not come though all the stars foretold otherwise. He is not the slave of the stars but their Maker. Is it not said in all the old stories that he is not a Tame Lion?"

"Well said, well said, Jewel," cried the King. "Those are the very words: *not a tame lion*. It comes in many tales."[3]

Tirian and Jewel understand what it means to say that Aslan is "not a tame lion." Aslan comes and goes as he pleases, but always for the good of Narnia and in ways consistent with the "deeper magic before the dawn of time." They have trouble understanding Aslan's apparent behavior, as they are told that "Aslan" has ordained the felling of the trees of Lantern Waste, thus killing the tree spirits within them. "Aslan" has also sold free Narnians and talking beasts into slavery to the Calormenes. The many tales they have heard about Aslan have led them to anticipate that they will be able to know, trust, and love him. They are now incredulous and heartbroken that the Aslan they once knew might sanction murder and slavery.

Their growing alarm leads Tirian and Jewel to investigate this terrible hearsay, and this eventually leads to their rash act of vengeance by the sword against two Calormenes whom they find mistreating a Narnian horse. Racked by remorse and guilt, they decide to turn themselves in to the authorities, to be dealt with by the new, ruthless Aslan so foreign to them:

> "He is not a *tame* lion," said Tirian. "How should we know what he would do? We, who are murderers. Jewel, I will go back. I will give up my sword and put myself in the hands of these Calormenes and ask that they bring me before Aslan. Let him do justice to me."[4]

Aslan now appears to be neither safe nor good, but the good king knows only one way to act. He is called upon to honor Aslan no matter how he appears. In his heart Tirian says, "Would it not be better to be dead than to have this horrible fear that Aslan has come and is not like the Aslan we have believed in and longed for? It is as if the sun rose one day and were a black sun."[5]

What he and Jewel discover, of course, is that these killing sprees and tales of bondage actually result from the devious plot of an Ape, fittingly named Shift. The Ape coerces his hapless donkey companion, Puzzle, to masquerade as Aslan in a ridiculous lion-skin costume. Thereafter, his role is to pretend to be Aslan in order to accomplish Shift's goal of taking over the whole realm of Narnia. This gambit creates a graphic image of how simple it is to use deceit and cunning to undermine thousands of years of education, training, and tradition, and of how easy it is for others to be taken in by appearances.

More than twenty-five hundred years have passed in Narnia time since Aslan created that world, but this has been equivalent to no more than fifty earth years. Narnia's cultural awareness has continued to ebb and flow. Embrace of the true Aslan has waned; and the freedom, health, and well-being of Narnia's citizens have diminished accordingly. Those who uphold their civilization and its underpinnings listlessly are easily seduced by demagogues who would steal their liberty and market it for power. Shift carefully situates Puzzle so that the Narnians never get a good look at him or hear him speak. Lewis thereby demonstrates that if we do not look beyond the surface and measure what our senses tell us against an unchanging standard, what we hope to be true and enduring will disappear. Shift uses the false, silent Aslan to make his own pronouncements credible and to exploit the now bewildered and oppressed citizens of Narnia. Little does Shift know the outcome of such pretensions of power and glory. As the Pevensie clan has experienced, there is always a faithful remnant in Narnia that will rally to restore true understanding.

These themes actively reflect Jesus' Parable of the Weeds from the Gospel of Matthew. Before the consummation of the age, evil coexists with good, awaiting final judgment:

> *"The kingdom of heaven is like a man who sowed good seed in his field. But while everyone was sleeping, his enemy came and sowed weeds among the wheat, and went away. When the wheat sprouted and formed heads, then the weeds also appeared.*
>
> *"The owner's servants came to him and said, 'Sir, didn't you sow good seed in your field? Where then did the weeds come from?'*
>
> *"'An enemy did this,' he replied.*
>
> *"The servants asked him, 'Do you want us to go and pull them up?'*

> " 'No,' he answered, 'because while you are pulling
> the weeds, you may root up the wheat with them. Let both
> grow together until the harvest. At that time I will tell
> the harvesters: First collect the weeds and tie them in
> bundles to be burned; then gather the wheat and bring it
> into my barn.' " MATTHEW 13:24-30

Lewis dramatizes the truth of this parable—how the weeds of mistrust work against faith—to show that good must do battle with evil until the very end and that evildoers will be dealt with decisively in the final harvest. *The Last Battle* shows how weeds of indifference and neglect can choke even willing believers and cause them to trade their certainties for doubts. Fear and unbelief triumph when people no longer know whom to trust. In the last days of Narnia, the challenge is to read the signs accurately and to trust in Aslan even when his public reputation is tarnished and imposters claim to speak for him.

TASH VS. ASLAN IN *THE LAST BATTLE*

Shift is shifty, clever, and manipulative. He is the enemy in the Parable of the Weeds who sows strife, hopelessness, and rebellion by perverting the truth. He also models the shift in Narnian culture away from Aslan and toward Tash, the evil god of the Calormenes. His transparent strategy is to appropriate old sayings to justify his treachery. The Narnians assembled before Shift demand to see and hear Aslan in person, since "in the old days, everyone could talk to him face to face."[6] Shift turns them aside:

> "Don't you believe it," said the Ape. "And even if it was true, times have changed. Aslan says he's been far too soft with you before, do you see? Well, he isn't going to be soft any more. He's going to lick you into shape this time. He'll teach you to think he's a tame lion!"[7]

What Shift says of Aslan does not ring true in the living memories of those who know the tales of the Lion King, but their fear is real. Perhaps they have unwittingly displeased Aslan and he is disciplining them, as is his right. Still, the Lamb cries out,

> "What have we to do with the Calormenes? We belong to Aslan. They belong to Tash. They have a god called Tash. They say he has four arms and the head of a vulture. They kill men on his altar. I don't believe there's any such person as Tash. But if there was, how could Aslan be friends with him?"[8]

Shift's clever, cynical tactic is to ridicule the Lamb's earnest question and to conflate Tash and Aslan into the same being:

> "Silly little bleater! Go home to your mother and drink milk. What do you understand of such things!

But you others, listen. Tash is only another name for Aslan. All that old idea of us being right and the Calormenes wrong is silly. We know better now. The Calormenes use different words but we all mean the same thing. Tash and Aslan are only two different names for You Know Who. That's why there can never be any quarrel between them. Get that into your heads, you stupid brutes. Tash is Aslan; Aslan is Tash."[9]

"Tashlan," as this syncretized deity comes to be called, represents the ultimate duplicity of false religion. Most of the Narnians we meet now are world weary and beaten down by rumor and doubt. When the false Aslan appears to the talking animals—shown to them only at a distance and in poor light—they lack discernment and, thus, the power to resist. Repeated enough times, and underwritten by the threat of force, citizens will eventually make no distinction between the two or, worse, despise both Aslans and debunk the prospect of trusting either of them.

The independent and prideful Ginger takes this one step further than Shift. As an atheist, Ginger believes in neither Tash nor Aslan; he finds a colleague in Rishda Tarkaan, a Calormene captain who agrees with Ginger that "*Aslan* means neither less nor more than *Tash*."[10] For them, religion is merely a means to an end, and that end is unholy power to enslave others to do their bid-

ding. The equating of Aslan with Tash is the final out-
rage that motivates Narnia's last king to recover as
much as he can about Aslan's history in Narnia.
Searching his heart and mind for a way to save Narnia,
he is fortified by his memory of Aslan's goodness and
care; he knows that Aslan would not countenance such
an evil arrangement or any truce with evil. But Tirian,
too, must overcome doubts as he contemplates the old
stories of help coming from the world of men: "But it
was all long ago. . . . That sort of thing doesn't happen
now." Still, he persists in a desperate launch of faith,
crying out, "Aslan! Aslan! Aslan! Come and help us
now. . . . If you will not come yourself, at least send me
the helpers from beyond the world. Or let me call them.
Let my voice carry beyond the world."[11]

Faithful to his word, Aslan answers, and Eustace
and Jill buoyantly return to untie Tirian. Together,
they move on to rescue Jewel and Puzzle, who join their
righteous cause. "Our citizenship is in heaven," Paul
says (Philippians 3:20), and citizenship carries obliga-
tions to our fellow citizens. To be Narnian, first and
foremost, is to know Aslan, recognize his voice, understand his character, and put everything under his authority. To be Narnian means to act justly, live nobly,
and esteem a Narnian neighbor as equal to oneself.

The breakdown of these common values is dramatized particularly by the dwarfs in Narnia. We remember the nefarious behavior of Nikabrik in *Prince Caspian*,

and now, in the last days of Narnia, we find that his descendent dwarfs have identified themselves as Narnia's official skeptics. They have marshaled their collective "wisdom" around the treasonous notion that there is no Aslan, or that if he does exist, he is merely the consolidation of other deities. Their signature motto, "The Dwarfs are for the Dwarfs," proclaims their solidarity. They don't care about the real Aslan; their question is, What does it matter? Their spokesman, the black dwarf Griffle, epitomizes their grim stance: "I don't know how all you chaps feel, but I feel I've heard as much about Aslan as I want to for the rest of my life."[12]

Tash, "the inexorable, the irresistible," is not Aslan's equal in any way, any more than Satan is God's counterpart in some dualistic universe. Rather, he is an underworld, demonic demigod, possessing a humanoid shape with four arms, a vulture head, and grotesque fingers with forbidding talons. He cannot bless, console, or save. He can only curse, punish, and damn. The religion of Tash as practiced in Calormen and as exported to Narnia by Shift and his cohorts is based on human sacrifice and vicious oppression. The society formed around Tash rewards violence, intimidation, and inequality enacted by menace and cruelty. Tash is not really worshipped, just feared; merciless tyrants use his name to induce terror. Shift foolishly clamors for his presence, even though he does not believe in such a deity. It is mere superstition to him, but practicing the dark arts and summoning evil spirits is not for amateurs, as he soon learns.

As the opposing sides reach Stable Hill, a setting as poignant as the Stone Table in *The Lion, the Witch, and the Wardrobe*, the valiant band of persevering Narnians plan to use facts about Aslan as their primary defense. Aslan and Tash are not the same, and Aslan is the true and loving King they have always been seeking. The Stable simultaneously represents birth and death; it is a way in and a way out. It is a portal to Aslan's country and, paradoxically, also Tash's shrine, a slaughterhouse for those offered up to Tash. For the evil Rishda, Ginger, and Shift, and those they push in, it is a fateful meeting place between them and their adopted demon, Tash.

The Stable is the final battleground, a place that is "far bigger inside than it was outside."[13] Inside the Stable, each finds his or her heart's desire. The unbelieving find the terrible Tash and final judgment. The true Narnians find Aslan—and with him, victory, peace, and joy. Tash, having performed his grisly duty, is forever banished by the decree of the Seven Kings and Queens of Narnia: "Begone, Monster, and take your lawful prey to your own place: in the name of Aslan and Aslan's great Father, the Emperor-over-the-Sea."[14]

In this final tale, Lewis echoes the "end times" theme found in the Bible, particularly in the last few books of the New Testament (2 Peter, Jude, Revelation). These prophecies predict a time near the end of life on earth in which humanity will face calamity and ruin. The confusion and wickedness of those "last days" will result in the judgment and destruction of the world, and a "New Heavens and Earth" that will replace the old and decayed version. According to the New Testament, Christ will then return to judge the living and the dead, rewarding the righteous and issuing justice to their enemies.

Readers of the New Testament are told that before Christ's return, false Christs and false prophets will appear (Matthew 24:24), including a particular "Antichrist." In a period of disorder and waning faith, these false Christs deceive people into believing that they are Christ in order to exploit their fears and enslave them. A false religion will evolve to substitute for the true one. The Antichrist is the false Christ who will set himself up as the supreme ruler of the planet. He will control human thought so that earthlings will believe falsehoods about themselves and about God. There are various interpretations of these themes, but as a "mere Christian," Lewis is not interested in expounding on them. Clearly, we are to see the parallel relationship between the false Aslan played by Puzzle and the true Aslan that Narnians have allowed to fade from their cultural memory. As we surmise from this tale, this is to their peril.

SUSAN AND EMETH IN *THE LAST BATTLE*

There are two unexpectedly poignant moments in *The Last Battle*, one that concerns a former friend of Narnia and one involving an avowed enemy. When Tirian is introduced to the humans who have arrived in response to his plaintive cry for help, he misses someone. " 'Sir,' said Tirian. . . . 'If I have read the chronicles aright, there should be another. Has not your Majesty two sisters? Where is Queen Susan?' "

Peter answers, "My sister Susan . . . is no longer a friend of Narnia."[15] Eustace, Jill, and Polly explain Susan's absence as due to a combination of personal vanity, popularity seeking, and premature "adulthood." Susan rejects opportunities to reminisce about Narnian adventures and regards them as "childish games" they played when they were younger. A profound sadness descends on the conversation, as each in turn realizes how grievously they feel her absence. Susan has gone her own way, keen on being grown-up, and has rejected the pathway between these two worlds ruled by Aslan.

There is a profound realism at work here that deserves some attention. Though the Chronicles are written as fairy tales, there is also what Lewis called "realism of presentation"; that is, that within the rules of the genre, the author provides a consistent window on the way that the creatures in the fantasy world behave, whether talking Horses, Apes, or human beings.[16] Susan is a Daughter of Eve, subject to all the vanities any young woman would face; she is also, for once and always, a Queen of Narnia. She is pulled between these two worlds, and she has apparently refused the fellowship of Narnia and chosen a different path. According to Lady Polly, "Her whole idea is to race on to the silliest time of one's life as quick as she can and then stop there as long as she can."[17]

In Susan's case, this seems to involve subjugation of the imagination to the practical reason of everyday life. It's time to get along with one's career, after all—we can't be children forever. Lewis is demonstrating that even under the reign of Aslan, one can turn away, temporarily or permanently forfeiting one's citizenship in Narnia. One must guard one's heart vigilantly on either side of the Wardrobe. Susan is not with the others in the railway accident that readers know has ended the earthly lives of the other Pevensies, Lord Digory, and Lady Polly and has brought them to Narnia for the last time. Her life is now irrevocably changed—how will she get on without her brothers and sister, cousins and friends? Her memories will change as well. We do not know her destiny, but we do know that Aslan will not abandon nor forsake her.

By contrast, the noble Calormene Emeth is a supposed enemy of Aslan who has spent his life in service to Tash. He alone, willingly and proactively, expresses his desire to meet Tash, for he is a sincere believer. Having only noble intentions and a pure heart, Emeth (whose name means "truth" in Hebrew) is welcomed inside the Stable not by the now departed Tash, but by King Aslan. Emeth is surprised to learn that in serving Tash, he has really been serving Aslan, whom he thought was his enemy (a judgment that only Aslan has the right to make): " 'Beloved,' said the Glorious One, 'unless thy desire had been for me thou wouldst not have sought so long and so truly. For all find what they truly seek.' "

That Emeth's heart has been set on his real King is evident in his stirring testimony: "It is better to see the Lion and die than to be Tisroc of the world and live and not to have seen him."[18]

Grace is getting credit for things one didn't do; mercy is not receiving blame for the things one has done. Emeth receives both grace and mercy. He finds his counterparts in two New Testament seekers who trust Jesus without question: the Roman centurion who asks Christ to heal his daughter and Cornelius, a Gentile believer seeking the true God that the apostle Peter is sent to teach and disciple. Both receive what they sought—healing and salvation—not because they had the right nationality or ethnic history but because they wished to meet the true God with all their hearts and were willing to trust him regardless of risk or rejection.

FAREWELL TO SHADOW-LANDS

We began our study of the Chronicles by focusing on C. S. Lewis's personal quest for joy and its impact on his fairy tales. *The Last Battle* shows us that the quest for joy must be a disinterested task: One is "surprised" by joy—it creeps up on one, as it did for Emeth. The seeker must not put it first, or he will miss both joy and its by-products—happiness, peace, and contentment shared in a community of comrades. In *The Last Battle*, this surprising and surpassing joy involves a certain tying up of loose ends, the promise of reunion with friends, and the final triumph of the good and the faithful. Digory, Lucy, Mr. Tumnus, and others reappear to "save" old Narnia once again, only to help preside over its death and rebirth. Lewis has given us a picture of the end times.

Lewis's concept of joy is intimately related to his view of history and how it unfolds; it is thus worth contemplating in this final chapter, as it informs his development of Narnian history as well. For Lewis, "life under the sun," as the writer of Ecclesiastes calls history, is linear. That is, it has a discernible beginning, middle, and end. This contrasts with a more cyclical view of history, whose proponents believe that repeating cycles and predictable patterns of events invariably and repeatedly result in the same effects. We are recycled or reincarnated, unable to get off the merry-go-round. This is not so—in our world or in Narnia.

Lewis's biblical view of history is different. Its premise is that history has an end in two senses of the word: as having a termination point and as having a purpose. Lewis's Christian faith taught him that the purpose of history is to reveal God's character and to demonstrate his justice and mercy. For those who discern that purpose and embrace God's justice and mercy, history's end is a joyful climax to human action and the eternal extension of that life in heaven. History does not just go on and on repeating itself. It comes to a stopping point at which evil is judged, the good are rewarded, and a permanent, glorious homeland awaits those who will live forever.

At the final judgment, depicted in *The Last Battle*, Aslan's followers are revealed for who they really are as they go through the door of the Stable. Within, they find immortality; a startling encounter with a world of unimagined beauty; and a bigger, more expansive landscape than they could ever have dreamed of:

> "'I see,' she said at last, thoughtfully. 'I see now. This garden is like the stable. It is far bigger inside than it was outside.'
>
> "'Of course, Daughter of Eve,' said the Faun. 'The further up and the further in you go, the bigger everything gets. The inside is larger than the outside.'"[19]

There has been a "Narnia inside Narnia" all along, waiting to be born—a Narnia that encompasses not only adventures in Aslan's world but in their own as well, for he is forever King of both.

When Aslan announces that "the dream is ended," he is declaring that the children and all the rest have died to the old realm, only to be ushered into an eternal landscape where the stories never end.[20] The Shadow-Lands, Lewis's image of the fallen world, beset by evil and in need of rescue and redemption, gives way to the New Narnia, where there is a joyful and enduring happy ending for all. Thus Lewis assembles all our favorites one more time in their royal garb for a curtain call that is really an invitation to remain forever. Beyond our wildest dreams, however satisfying our adventures in our own time and place, lies a destiny that is more glorious and joyful than we could possibly imagine. Lewis calls upon his readers to see the present as a mere shadow compared to the bright reality of what is prepared for them beyond Narnia.

The sweet reunion of beloved friends—characters with whom we have traveled far and wide in Narnia, Archenland, Calormen, and on earth—is one of the greatest treasures in *The Last Battle*. Lewis, and most of us, long to see loved ones who have passed into the next world. It is reassuring and comforting to see such characters as Lord Digory and Lady Polly once again. For Lewis, eternity is a place where we gather with friends, loved ones, family, and comrades, all in the presence of Aslan, extending the stories of our adventures in the peaceful, joyful context of a world in which righteousness reigns.

In these words from the "Heaven" chapter of *The Problem of Pain*, Lewis gives powerful testimony to the longing we have been tracing throughout Narnia and which finds its climax in *The Last Battle*. It explains the source of our homesickness and the remedy for our restless hearts:

> This signature on each soul may be a product of heredity and environment, but that only means that heredity and environment are among the instruments whereby God creates a soul. . . . Your soul has a curious shape because it is a hollow made to fit a particular swelling in the infinite contours of the Divine substance, or a key to unlock one of the doors in the house with many mansions. For it is not humanity in the abstract that is to be saved, but you, the individual reader, John Stubbs or Janet Smith. Blessed and fortunate creature, your eyes shall behold Him and not another's. All that you are, sins apart, is destined, if you will let God have His good way, to utter satisfaction. . . . Your place in heaven will seem to be made for you and you alone, because you were made for it—made for it stitch by stitch as a glove is made for a hand.[21]

We long for this homecoming, and *The Last Battle* can help us visualize that day. Our courage to seek it is restored and our vision to see it renewed. Lewis's fairy

tales—like his apologetics, literary criticism, and poetry—exude just this sort of personalized hope. They
manifest the generous and earnest spirit God gave him
to lift readers out of their protective selfishness and to
welcome them into a partnership of joyful discovery.
Lewis's genius is in reminding us of events yet to take
place that are as real and significant as those that have
already passed us by. This future in New Narnia is
worth clinging to; it will indeed be a place made for us
because we were made for it.

EPILOGUE

AFTER NARNIA

Our lifelong nostalgia, our longing to be reunited with something in the universe from which we now feel cut off, to be on the inside of some door which we have always seen from the outside, is no mere neurotic fancy, but the truest index of our real situation.[1]

C. S. LEWIS, *TRANSPOSITION AND OTHER ADDRESSES*

SUGGESTED READINGS:

The Lion, the Witch, and the Wardrobe: chapter 5
The Voyage of the "Dawn Treader": chapter 14

We have traversed the moral and spiritual landscape of Narnia, we have told and retold the stories to ourselves, and we are now in a position to explain easily to others why we can continue to learn from Aslan. Under his reign, we are free to imagine and indwell a spiritual realm that has reawakened in us the desire for goodness, the presence of hope, and the longing for joy. This is, as Lewis says in the epigraph, "no mere neurotic fancy, but the truest index of our real situation." To imagine and sustain hope in a world we cannot see but which is, in fact, more real than our own is Lewis's legacy, the gift of Aslan.

But there comes a time when Aslan will also say to us what he has said to Peter and Susan, Lucy and Edmund—it is time to leave Narnia and "go closer to our world." We fear losing him, but that will not happen. He is here, in our world and in all worlds. What is life like after Narnia? How do we go "further up and further in" on our side of the Wardrobe?

RE-ENCHANTING OUR COSMOS

Lewis and his work now span three centuries—the one in which he was born, the one in which he lived most of his life, and the present one, in which his writings live on. He is still informing conversations as to the best ways of understanding and presenting the faith to the wayward and the searching. Lewis aspired to be a student of all centuries but a permanent resident of none. Freed from having to believe that the latest is always the best, or the newest always the truest, Lewis could anchor his vocation, his faith, and his life in something other than newspaper headlines or the vagaries of modern science.

Lewis knew that his fellow Westerners needed a vantage point that was safely outside of themselves—objective, unbiased, and uninvested with their own ambitions and preferences. He learned, like Peter, Lucy, Edmund, Eustace, Jill, Polly, Digory, and countless others who have visited Narnia, that this perspective can come only from Aslan's country. Lewis remains our wise navigator well into the twenty-first century precisely because, like the ancient men of Issachar, he "understood [his own] times and knew what to do" (1 Chronicles 12:32).

We, too, must understand our times. Through the eyes of the Sons of Adam and Daughters of Eve, we regain sight of the paths we must take, confident of where they will lead us. That requires, as we well know, cultivating a disciplined imagination as well as our powers of logical reasoning. Both are defenses against the stultifying naturalism that co-opts reason for its own campaign against heaven and reduces the imagination to wishful thinking. We know better.

Imagination is sometimes juxtaposed with reason, or opposed to it, even in Christian contexts. In many discussions, one trumps the other, so as we meditate on our extended stay in Narnia, it is worth examining the role of both in Lewis's apologetics and fiction and how they interact. As we have observed, reason and imagination are held in useful, creative tension in Narnia, given Lewis's romantic worldview. This tension is especially well articulated in his short essay, "Meditation in a Toolshed."[2] In it, Lewis relabels reason and imagination as "looking at" and "looking along." "Looking at," in Lewis's shorthand, is the scientific view that is detached, impersonal, and objective, the outsider's view led by reason and driven by facts. It is epitomized by disinterested inductive reasoning and highlighted by purportedly value-free, dispassionate, nonpartisan description. "Looking along," by contrast, is the nonscientific view, the participatory, personal, and subjective insider view led by experience and driven by the imagination. It is characterized by invested, proactive commitment to the object or person known, without the pretense of indifference or the claim of nonbias. Lewis illustrates these stances vividly in this passage:

> The mathematician sits thinking, and to him it seems that he is contemplating timeless and spaceless truths about quantity. But the cerebral physiologist, if he could look inside the mathematician's head, would find nothing timeless and spaceless there—only tiny movements in the grey matter. The savage dances in

ecstasy at midnight before Nyonga and feels with every muscle that his dance is helping to bring the new green crops and the spring rain and the babies. The anthropologist, observing that savage, records that he is performing a fertility ritual of the type so-and-so. The girl cries over her broken doll and feels that she has lost a real friend; the psychologist says that her nascent maternal instinct has been temporarily lavished on a bit of shaped and coloured wax.[3]

The mathematician, the savage, and the little girl are "looking along"; the physiologist, anthropologist, and psychologist are "looking at." Who is experiencing or reporting the truth about their respective situations? Lewis's answer in the essay is that each case must be reviewed on its own merits, and that both "looking at" and "looking along" are essential components of a healthy intellect and crucial to negotiating the world with wisdom and hope. This is certainly the case in Narnia.

In *The Voyage of the "Dawn Treader,"* Ramandu, the "retired star," responds to Eustace's largely innocent but narrow-minded comment that "in our world . . . a star is a huge ball of flaming gas," with this gentle rebuke: "Even in your world, my son, that is not what a star is but only what it is made of."[4] Eustace is a victim of his constrictive, "looking at" kind of vision; he needs to "look along," as Narnians do, or he will miss the point entirely. By contrast, when Lucy's report of having been through the Wardrobe and into Narnia is dismissed by her brothers and sister, Professor Kirke deftly uses logic and reason to unpack their bias and champion Lucy's credibility. "Looking at" her character allows her siblings to "look along" her experience and embrace both.

In our world, both looking "at" and "along" accompany every true act of comprehension; they assist us in seeing that some things can be neither/nor or both/and. But Lewis is concerned in this essay, and elsewhere, with more than just illustrating healthy intellects and prescribing the proper mediation between reason and imagination. He hopes, rather, to expose the modern tendency (by which he means since the Enlightenment) to privilege one way of knowing—"looking at"—over the other.

> The answer is that we must never allow the [privileging] to begin. We must, on pain of idiocy, deny from the very outset the idea that looking *at* is, by its own nature, intrinsically truer or better than looking *along*. One must look both along and at everything. In particular cases we shall find reason for regarding the one or the other vision as inferior.[5]

When "looking at" becomes enfranchised as the exclusive way of understanding oneself and the world, or the official genre of knowing and reporting what is true, the unintended and unremarked consequence is to empty

both the cosmos and humankind of the supreme spiritual significance each once had. This emptying occurs
chiefly by stealing or suspending the "grand narrative"
that once made human beings the crown of creation,
made in God's image. In Genesis, we read of the original enchantment, the primeval but true reality. Robbed
of divine fellowship by the Fall, men and women now
also lose their humanity to scientism—science not as
method but as god. This unwarranted secular deity is
entrenched in contemporary Western intellectual circles. As Lewis carefully explains it,

> The process whereby man has come to know the
> universe is from one point of view extremely compli-
> cated, from another it is alarmingly simple. We can
> observe a single one-way progression. At the outset
> the universe appears packed with will, intelligence,
> life and positive qualities; every tree is a nymph and
> every planet a god. Man himself is akin to the gods.
> The advance of knowledge gradually empties this
> rich and genial universe: first of its gods, then of its
> colours, smells, sounds and tastes, finally of solidity
> itself as solidity was originally imagined. As these
> items are taken from the world, they are transferred
> to the subjective side of the account: classified as our
> sensations, thoughts, images or emotions. The Sub-
> ject becomes gorged, inflated, at the expense of the
> Object. But the matter does not rest there.[6]

Lewis is pointing out the ironies of what in our day is common establishment thinking about theological and supernatural phenomena. While our ancestors could speak of God, angels, and the possibility of divine encounters as objective fact, these topics have been reduced to the category of the subjective as wishful thinking. But there are no brakes for stopping this reductionist machine.

> The same method which has emptied the world now proceeds to empty ourselves. The masters of the method soon announce that we were just as mistaken (and mistaken in much the same way) when we attributed "souls" or "selves" or "minds" to human organisms, as when we attributed Dryads to the trees. Animism, apparently, begins at home. We, who have personified all other things, turn out to be ourselves mere personifications. Man is indeed akin to the gods: that is, he is no less phantasmal than they. Just as the Dryad is a "ghost," an abbreviated symbol for all the facts we know about the tree foolishly mistaken for a mysterious entity over and above the facts, so the man's "mind" or "consciousness" is an abbreviated symbol for certain verifiable facts about his behaviour: a symbol mistaken for a thing. And just as we have been broken of our bad habit of personifying trees, so we must now be broken of our habit of personifying man.[7]

The final outcome of such "depersonification" is what we observed earlier as a "disenchanted cosmos." A world that formerly regarded a fact as something "objectively true" now blithely ascribes "facthood" to mere subjectivity, reducing the claim of truth to a matter of personal opinion or assertion—or who has the most votes. We may have thought that only a few Dryads, ghosts, and talking trees were at stake; in the end, it is the very humanity of men and women, their uniqueness among creatures, their place in the Creator's universe that has been drained away in the onslaught against the imagination. This is the work of the Queen of the Underland writ large. Are there Puddleglums among us to stand against it?

A disenchanted existence destroys the familiar order and structure of the world as God narrated it; displaces its cast of characters, its themes, its beginning, middle, and end; and substitutes a story alien to its foundations and to its sense of being and belonging. In this tale, neither God nor humankind has a speaking part, and the "grand narrative" gives way to the "grand mechanism." This agentless, authorless story has supplanted Christianity and virtually all religious paradigms in Western education over the last seventy-five years. It has even overcome the cult of the humanities, art, and poetry by establishing as its sacred text Charles Darwin's *On the Origin of Species*. Its key doctrine is natural selection, and its holy sacrament, progress.

Put slightly differently, the multiple plot lines of the ancient and medieval world so loved by Lewis and Tolkien—tales of gods and men, sin and rebellion, fatal flaws and redemption, epochs and eras that define virtue and denounce vice, premodern myths that shaped and governed the cultures and civilizations before the Enlightenment and that still shape and govern those regions and villages immune to the secular West's contagion—have been reduced to one modern monomyth. This reigning narrative is an inexorable, impersonal process that depicts only the wordless, frameless, temporary ascent of one species, ironically still suffering from the illusion that there is such a thing as human volition, human dignity, and human destiny. The fiercely unbelieving desperately embrace the evolutionary monomyth, thinking that it saves them from the problem of explaining our unique personhood. Walker Percy has captured this madness well: "The modern objective consciousness will go to any length to prove that it is not unique in the Cosmos, and by this very effort establishes its own uniqueness. Name another entity in the Cosmos which tries to prove it is not unique."[8]

When a society succumbs to such a lowly state and such a poor estimation of human worth, it has left itself few options. If "grand narrative" denotes the premodern world of myths and multiple stories that Christianity edits and weaves together into its own grandest narrative, and if "grand mechanism" denotes the prevailing modernist worldview created by scientism, then "grand delusion" seems an apt description of the status quo. The post-postmodern Western world, rejecting earlier enchantments including the Darwinian monomyth we've just described, clings only by tenacious nostalgia to the hope that there may be a home awaiting them on some peaceful shore.

With neither heaven nor science to guide us, we elect "whatever" to give shape to our lives, even if it is the mirage that we can make up our story as we go along: my world and welcome to it. My story doesn't have to connect to anything; I will live it out, one day at a time, without regard to its having ultimate purpose, because any value it has is only what I invest it with. My PDA is my bible; there's always one more meeting or task or appointment in my desk calendar to keep me distracted. The sad progression is from multiple stories to the true story, to its rejection and supplanting by the false story, to no story at all. Thus we uncover the depths of our disenchantment and our need for recovery. We need re-enchantment.

NARNIAN APOLOGETICS

Fortunately for us, Aslan is still on the move. Narnia has its own apologetics, its defense of the ways of God to man, centered in the being of Aslan. Lewis explained it this way:

Let us *suppose* that there were a land like Narnia and that the Son of God, as He became a Man in our world, became a Lion there, and then imagine what would happen.[9]

Indeed, imagine the reverse. What would happen if Aslan crossed over into our world! But, of course he has, and when Lewis came to Christ, but arguably even before that, he grounded his thinking in a transcendent view that would make sense of this world and the next. He adopted the perspective of eternity, that "all that is not eternal is eternally out of date," not the court of public opinion or the cult of private feeling.[10] Aslan alone would guide his curricular choices, his scholarly production, the themes of his public addresses, and even the genres of his fiction. He had been prepared by Providence his whole life to write fairy tales:

> I saw how stories of this kind could steal past a certain inhibition which had paralysed much of my own religion in childhood. Why did one find it so hard to feel as one was told one ought to feel about God or about the sufferings of Christ? I thought the chief reason was that one was told one ought to. An obligation to feel can freeze feelings. And reverence itself did harm. . . . But supposing that by casting all these things into an imaginary world, stripping them of their stained-glass and Sunday school associations, one could make them for the first time appear in their

real potency? Could one not thus steal past those watchful dragons?[11]

Apologetics is really just a fancy word for "stealing past watchful dragons." Lewis did that tirelessly on behalf of Christ, not only in his fiction, but everywhere. He exemplified a responsible and compelling way to take a stand, articulate a position, clarify and extend arguments convincingly, translate and amplify meanings to diverse groups, make difficult concepts easy to understand, and above all build bridges to skeptical or indifferent audiences by taking pains to see the world through their eyes first, not as we would wish them to see. Narnia is one such bridge built toward one such audience in need of hope.

The apostle Peter tells us to be ready always to give an answer for the hope that is in us (see 1 Peter 3:15). That is a good description of what Lewis accomplishes in the Chronicles of Narnia, tales that are filled with profound hope, especially when things look bleakest. Frankly, what makes Lewis effective in the twenty-first century has little to do with what most of us think of first. It is not the formidable skill of philosophical argumentation, the considerable lucidity of his prose, or the legendary perspicacity of his reading and scholarship. Rather, what makes him effective is that he knew what it meant to be lost; therefore he made it his life's purpose to explore, fathom, and express the reason for the hope within him using story, image, and symbol. He served the King of kings not only with his prodigious intellect but with his broken and restored heart and his unfailing empathy with the lost.

Joseph told his brothers, "You intended to harm me, but God intended it for good to accomplish what is now being done, the saving of many lives" (Genesis 50:20). So Lewis can say (to his earthly father): "When you abandoned me, you bequeathed me the bitter inheritance of feeling lost, homeless, displaced, stranded, exiled, fatherless—a pilgrim in this world—but God has transformed this terror into good." Lewis forgave Albert as he embraced his Savior. If, when he reflected on the aftermath of his mother's death, "it was all sea and islands," these became all hope and glory for the Lewis who was being rescued.[12] Lewis did not just know this intellectually as "Oxford's bonny fighter," but as a son; he knew what it meant to long for news from home, from Father. What the lost need is hope.

After his conversion, everything Lewis wrote was marked by his vibrant hope, and it is found on every page of the Chronicles. Lewis pursued joy intensely in his private struggles, and he eventually found hope in surrender, in a supernatural recovery from the despair, isolation, and loneliness of his early life. His life mirrors the experience of all of us at least sometime in our lives, whether in adolescence or adulthood. Lewis knew what it meant to be lost, and he knew what it meant to write stories that helped others to find hope.

As apologist and mythmaker, Lewis teaches us that hope comes first, and after it come the reasons for hope. Narnia does not capture us with safe platitudes but by the mane of a dangerously good Lion, a ferocious, wild, untamable Beast who loves us enough to lay down his life. We must never forget the bitter and confusing lostness, the isolation and spiritual barrenness by which the unsaved and the unenlightened negotiate the world. Paul describes this condition eloquently and succinctly as being "without hope and without God in the world" (Ephesians 2:12). That well described Lewis's predicament (and our own) before we found the way home.

Theology professor Peter Kreeft of Boston College, one of the best expositors of Lewis's legacy, has called this insight of Lewis's the "argument from desire," and I call it the "appeal to homesickness." Our desire is to come home, to affirm that the great Captain of our souls has gone to prepare a place for us, that where he is, we shall be also (see John 14:2-3).

> "Do fish complain of the sea for being wet? Or if they did, would that fact itself not strongly suggest that they had not always been, or would not always be, purely aquatic creatures? If you are really a product of a materialistic universe, how is it that you don't feel at home there?"[13]

As this quotation suggests, Lewis awakens the joy, the search, the hope in those who read his stories, comb his essays, and respond to his welcoming, endearing voice. But his achievement is perhaps even more profound than that.

The testimony of many of Lewis's readers is that he has not just identified a longing or a God-shaped vacuum already present but has helped to create the longing itself. One can hardly read the Narnia Chronicles or the Space Trilogy or *Till We Have Faces* without encountering a father, a brother, a sister, or a home that has been denied us in this world. You can hear it echoing in this passage from *The Problem of Pain*:

> The settled happiness and security which we all desire, God withholds from us by the very nature of the world: but joy, pleasure, and merriment He has scattered broadcast. We are never safe, but we have plenty of fun, and some ecstasy. It is not hard to see why. The security we crave would teach us to rest our hearts in this world and oppose an obstacle to our return to God: a few moments of happy love, a landscape, a symphony, a merry meeting with our friends, a bathe, or a football match, have no such tendency. Our Father refreshes us on the journey with some pleasant inns, but will not encourage us to mistake them for home.[14]

Yes, that's it. There is a longing deep, deep within us, a call resonating in our innermost being that tells us that we were made for eternity, that our identity, purpose, and destiny originate elsewhere than on this fallen planet or within our own limited imaginations. Narnia answers that call, prepares the way, secures our response. Throughout the Chronicles we learn that the greatest predicate is to know as we are known (see 1 Corinthians 13:12). Aslan teaches us anew that we are sought by the very God who created us, who knows our deepest longings, countenances our most lavish dreams, and relieves our most nagging fears. We are not to be rejected or renounced. Like the father of the Prodigal Son when he saw his boy coming home, our Father, who is Emperor-beyond-the-Sea, is running, leaping to meet us before we are even inside the gates.

That is the enduring effect of the Chronicles and of all Lewis's writing: to renew in us the hope of glory and to lead us beyond hope into saving faith and the security of our adoption as sons and daughters. In the words of the writer to the Hebrews:

> *The people in days of old . . . agreed that they were for-eigners and nomads here on earth. Obviously people who say such things are looking forward to a country they can call their own. If they had longed for the country they came from, they could have gone back. But they were looking for a better place, a heavenly homeland. That is why God is not ashamed to be called their God, for he has prepared a city for them.* HEBREWS 11:2, 13-16, NLT

Lewis re-enchants the cosmos—and isn't this what the apostle Peter has been saying all along is our job?

> *But in your hearts set apart Christ as Lord. Always be prepared to give an answer to everyone who asks you to give the reason for the hope that you have. But do this with gentleness and respect, keeping a clear conscience, so that those who speak maliciously against your good behavior in Christ may be ashamed of their slander.*
>
> 1 PETER 3:15-16

Evangelism, telling the Good News, is about giving people hope, an alternate history, a new cosmos, a new story, and the promise of a homeland that awaits us.

This is not about people who take apologetics courses or read difficult books about the problem of evil. It's not even about people who read books by or about C. S. Lewis. It is about giving an answer—your personal answer—to the questions people have about the reason for the hope they perceive in you. Never before has someone like you—with all your unique, God-given characteristics—submitted himself or herself to Christ. What mission does Christ have for you? Isn't that the enduring message of our encounter with Aslan? He has been calling you, waiting for you, so that he can inhabit and animate you to accomplish his purpose here on earth.

People who ask about hope are not yet asking about

reasons; hope is what they want to hear about. How can one believe in such a way as to have such hope? How can one behave in such a way that hope is made visible? How can one tell—and live—stories that open people's eyes to wonder and faith?

The Philippian jailer whose story is told in Acts 16 wasn't thinking of "The Four Spiritual Laws" as his world fell apart, and the answer Paul gave him was designed to bring hope, not more questions. "Believe in the Lord Jesus, and you will be saved" (Acts 16:31). That is the key.

Sometimes reasons are hard to come by. Hope goes deeper than reason. As Blaise Pascal, the great eighteenth-century mathematician said, "The heart has its reasons, which reason does not know."[15] The hope of which 1 Peter 3:15-16 speaks requires that we use every one of the gifts and talents God has given us to call one another home. I believe that this is how Lewis understood Peter's meaning, and he then infused it into the heart of the Narnian landscape. And this is why we are still listening to him today.

LEWIS REDUX

Reading and rereading the Chronicles over the years has encouraged me to wonder what it would have been like to have a private audience with Lewis. Oh, to ask him directly the questions burning in my heart! How might he have answered the challenges to faith that are being posed in our day? What advice would he have given me? Would I find him just as cogent and incisive as he was in the very last words he wrote?

It was thus that I found myself wandering in cyberspace one evening, traveling in an expectant but vaguely melancholy mood, despairing over my captivity to narrow horizons and shallow dreams, pushed on by my own deep longing to know and to believe . . . and then, there it was, one of those instant messenger pop-up windows, tucked away in the corner of my computer screen. As you can imagine, I was intrigued by the message: *Jack invites you to a conversation.*

"Jack"? What joker is playing around online tonight?

Against my better judgment, I typed in a reply: *Jack? Who are you? Where did you get my screen name?*

I've been shaken by the ensuing dialogue ever since. It went something like this . . .

LEWIS: Jack Lewis, here. Is that you, Bruce?

EDWARDS: Jack Lewis? As in Clive Staples Lewis? Yes, this is Professor Edwards—I mean, Bruce . . .

LEWIS: Bruce—how the deuce are you? I am afraid my clumsy fingers can't get used to this detestable keyboard! Don't be too impatient. My brother always did my typing for me, and he's off writing a new history of French politics. Say, I've been watching you and enjoying your video experiment.

My video experiment? How would a random chat-room denizen, even one with an overactive imagination, know that I have just spent the better part of a year trying to script a documentary on C. S. Lewis's life? Well, maybe if I play along with the charade . . .

EDWARDS: My what? Oh, you mean my documentary on Lewis—I mean, my documentary on you . . . ? Well, Jack, I'm weathering it—so much travel, and those blasted administrative chores I've taken on, but no matter. Hey, as long as you're online, I have a few things I'd like to seek your counsel on, if you don't mind.

LEWIS: Online? Oh, quite. We have some freedom here, you know, to peek in, have a look, and occasionally to weigh in, like tonight. I've taken a particular interest in you.

EDWARDS: Uhhh . . . Well, I'm flattered. But where's "here," Jack? "Freedom"? "Peek in"? What campus are you on?

LEWIS: Campus? Oh, I'm done with schools and schooling, Bruce. I graduated nearly forty-two years ago.

Wow, this guy is good, but what's his game? I need to keep playing along to see what he's up to.

EDWARDS: Well, Jack, since you're peeking in and all, I suppose you've noticed that you're still very

popular. Catholics and Protestants alike read you—
why, some "fundevangelicals" hardly read any other
Christian writers besides you.

LEWIS: Wait up, old chap. The what?

EDWARDS: The *fundevangelicals*—a neologism I coined
to describe . . .

LEWIS: Be careful, Bruce; you know what the Great
Knock would say: sloppy categorization, lumping
everybody into one camp for the purpose of dismiss-
ing them—a dangerous habit of mind. Here, old man,
every individual creature is uniquely loved, known,
specified in its creaturehood. You remember the old
nominalist debates—is each thing a particular or a
universal? Well, here the problem is solved.

EDWARDS: How so?

LEWIS: All are particulars . . .

EDWARDS: But how . . . ?

LEWIS: . . . and all are universals. There's no distinction. Each of us is *sui generis*, one of a kind. All along,
that's how God imagined us. Once you get here
(which is not a place, exactly, but an order or dimen-
sion of being that cannot be fathomed by mortal folk),
it will be immediately and spontaneously clear. My
Great Divorce wasn't so far off!

Bruce, when God "imagines," it's not like human daydreaming, for with him an "image" becomes concrete, or should I say "manifest"? *Concrete* is one of those words that makes little sense to a departed soul. Concrete compared with what? This is true reality, as solid and dense and "here" as any existence could be—just like, you'll recall, in *Perelandra* when the Green Lady . . .

EDWARDS: Look, sorry, Jack, I—I—appreciate the distance between us—literally—

LEWIS: "Literally!" As if anything on earth could be anything but a metaphor for the kind of being, the kind of transcendent reality that returnees like me experience! Why, I—

Who is this guy? I realized I was beginning to be drawn in, that I was taking this very seriously—much too seriously. I was talking to him as if he were really C. S. Lewis. *This guy is more than merely an impersonator. Maybe this trick question will draw him out. . . .*

EDWARDS: Okay, just tell me something, Jack. Is Christianity the one true religion? What about America, will it survive this century? And Western culture itself, is it destined to disintegrate?

LEWIS: Bruce, I can't answer those questions.

EDWARDS: "Can't?" Why not? Who's better to—?

LEWIS: Well, it's not that I *can't* answer them; in fact, I can, quite easily. I do so numerous times in my work—as you well know. But, well, to answer them in the way you have posed them here, with the proto-typically egocentric, ultimately definitive, historically encompassing perspective, etc., etc., would do neither you nor your students any good.

Drat, Bruce! I've not used the *etcetera* since I left Terra; it's not a concept that makes any sense here; *et al* doesn't work here, either; there's no "and so on" in heaven. Everything is specifically and exactly what it is and nothing else. To carelessly consign items and beings to any form of ellipsis is the essence of that other realm below, where nothing is what it is, and no body and no thing exists in itself. Hell is one long etcetera.

EDWARDS: Really, Jack. I think you're dodging my questions. They are straightforward—aren't they?

LEWIS: Wait, Bruce—all questions are situated in some context or other; they don't spring from a pure or static mode of being so that they can be answered prescriptively in the way humans think; to call your question, or any other, "straightforward" is to grant it the ultimacy of being that only God himself possesses.

EDWARDS: No straight answer from you, I see. Is there some "oath of secrecy" you've had to subscribe to since you left?

LEWIS: If I didn't know you better—though the truth is, I don't know you very well at all, dear chap—but judging from your tone, I'd say you are becoming quite sarcastic.

Don't you see that you're accusing me of what they accused your Elder Brother of when he became planetary? "No straight answers," they said. "Always answering questions with questions." Nearly every earnest query was met by a story of some sort to be interpreted by the hearer at his peril. You humans—you're so, so—

EDWARDS: Preoccupied with our own importance and a false sense of urgency?

LEWIS: Well, that, too, but what I was going to say is that you fashion a world and the rules for it from the crib, and then spend most of your lives asking why people and events don't conform to the rules you've made up. That's my biography, too, mind you.

EDWARDS: Now, hold on—you were an advocate of "mere Christianity" when you were "planetary," and—

LEWIS: Indeed, and I still am for those still in exile—like you. Up here, we don't talk about Christianity or religion as if it were a system of thought or a philosophical argument. We actually don't talk about Christianity as such at all. There's no "religion" here.

Just God's eternal Trinitarian presence: Father, Son, and Holy Ghost.

My good man, who needs to label or codify "systems" of thought when your very mode of existence makes unnecessary the need for separating things into dualities: mind/body, soul/spirit, male/female—all your (what did you call them?) "structuralist dichotomies." (Descartes and Kant and Leibniz, bless them, lived in a very small universe!)

EDWARDS: You mean that heaven transcends all our distinctions and categories?

LEWIS: If by "transcend" you mean "divests us of them," then, yes; but understand, now, those were never the qualities or identifying features that "individualized" or made any creature unique in the first place.

EDWARDS: If not them, then what?

LEWIS: Christ in you, the hope of glory, the divine spark, the eternal life—infinitely precious, and ultimately unique, because no greater being can be conceived of than God, the greatest of all "knowers."

Ultimate Mind, which is to say, Ultimate Spirit, Ultimate Person; each creature, therefore, bears the artistry of the Creator in a manner—form and content—that is utterly "one." You are "like" God, utterly so—and, also, that is, utterly "many"—utterly distinctive, yet different from all the other creatures made, yet known to and made known by him in a manner suited only to you. What you call existence is maintained by his holding you in a contemplation that never fails.

I can assure you, Bruce, there's never been anyone like you before or after; but don't get too puffed up— it's that way with us all! You cannot fathom the infinite diversity of the Creation—he positively revels in it. Your kind, all of you, would be scandalized by it on Terra—your notions of diversity are so limited!

Oh, to be known and to know—these are the ultimate predicates, just as I and Thou are the ultimate Subjects. Thus—

EDWARDS: Jack, you are making me believe my questions are trivial, or worse.

LEWIS: Trivial? Well, all merely human endeavor is penultimate, subordinate, temporal—as it was designed to be, after all. When you come to face your true self-hood, as I have, as all of us departed have, you come to think of your planetary, terran life as pure preparation, each self-deluded "serious" pursuit as having been something more like a game or an adventure, whose principles and exploits were to be understood and mastered as a discipline rather than merely endured— or, worse, escaped from, games and adventures that, since Eden, he would use to bring you home.

EDWARDS: So much suffering, such violence, such exploitation, tsunamis, cancer, war—how dare you call human life a game! That so sanitizes the subject.

LEWIS: "Sanitizes?" You mean, as if God had turned his back on humankind and creation? I didn't say human life is a game; in fact, I said from certain heavenly vantage points, one's former planetary preoccupation with the self and its satisfactions looms as an elaborate game or adventure.

"Sanitizes?" Are you a deist? The whole point of the Incarnation—and this is really elementary, Bruce, and I'm surprised to have to point it out—is to restore to wholeness the very fallen, very barren planetary life you caricature with glib abstractions—that's what suffering, violence, and exploitation are to you in the prosperous West. But his incarnate life did more than that; it demonstrated what true humanity is to be. Our Elder Brother underwent any and all the suffering, violence, and exploitation that humans can concoct—that's what was poured out into and onto him on the cross. "He who knew no sin was made to be sin. . . ." In his sojourn, his death, and his resurrection, he identified, condemned, and, if may I say it, outlived the rebellion that spread your corrupt humanism originally (emanating from Adam on down), and in its place portrayed real manhood—that is, loving, compassionate, merciful personhood.

He is the man that Adam was meant to be and wasn't. The Gospels' depiction of how he related to women and womanhood is unparalleled in ancient literature, you know. He came as a man and not as a woman, not to privilege one gender, but to deprivilege it, the whole category. "There is neither male, nor female. . . ." My dear sir, do you think God is a chauvinist?

EDWARDS: I don't know what I think. You've got me twisting and twirling, Jack. You're no help.

LEWIS: Sorry, old chap, truly sorry. But, it's all to the good. Twirl if you must, but when you stop, stop on stable ground. You ask whether this or that *ism* will survive. Planetary life was never—and heavenly life prohibitively is not—about isms. There aren't any sociologists in heaven, no poll takers, no spin doctors.

There are some "smart ones" here, but they quickly give up their pretensions of erudition. Heaven, you see, strips us not only of our vices but of our virtues as well—as Flannery O'Connor has reminded not a few of us here!

EDWARDS: In the end, then, none of this matters— my Lewis film and Narnian scholarship, the fate of American culture or the West, my students' aspirations. You're saying, "All is vanity"?

LEWIS: You'll remember this from your vast reading of my puny body of work, but let me quote myself to you: "All that is not eternal is eternally out of date."

What is eternal? What did your Elder Brother point to: faith, hope, and love?

Nothing is ultimately vain—even your "fundevangelicalism"—if it somehow contributes to the initiation or imitation of faith, hope, and love, especially the latter, for that's what God is: Love. Love incognito at times; Love as painful truth, occasionally; but Love, nevertheless.

Even your so-called fundevangelicals witness to this in their own faltering way. Because, you see, there only exist faltering ways—partial, time-bound, paradoxical, elusive. You can never, from Terra, fully explain or understand any phenomenon, even yourself. Only he can do that because he's been both inside and outside your world.

EDWARDS: Then it doesn't matter what view I take, what behavior I adopt? It's all the same? Liberal or conservative, believer or unbeliever, devout or skeptic?

LEWIS: There's the epitome of humanness for you— always either/or, dichotomous, antiparadoxical. Believe me, I understand it—I was a master of the dichotomy and the trichotomy while I labored "under the sun." (Remember "Liar, Lunatic, or Lord"?) But what I immediately discovered here is that heavenly truth is always paradoxical, but by the same token, always true.

Conformed to the real. To answer your question, Bruce, it matters a great deal. It matters eternally.

EDWARDS: Matters? Matters how? Circles within circles. I feel as if I am trapped in a kaleidoscope.

LEWIS: Now there's a useful metaphor: kaleidoscopic. That's planetary life for you. You just trace out one design and follow its linkage to another, and by the time you comprehend it, it's changed, by colour, contour, or their combination.

EDWARDS: There's no compass, then . . .

LEWIS: To the contrary. Revelation, reason, experience, God speaking through events, persons, texts—all are useful maps. But don't confuse the maps for the landscapes themselves—the Destination itself, I should say. You would have God spare us the journey, the negotiation, the navigation. Why do you think he speaks to us in dreams and deeds, in words and wonder? Is not the biblical record *true?* Of course. But is it easy to believe and trust? Of course not, for you must have your own encounter with him. Should his presence and the path to him be clearer? Clearer to whom, my dear chap?

Those who have eyes to see, see, and those who have ears to hear, hear. It's not his way, you know, confounding and dismaying as it may seem on Terra, to make sure that all things are always crystal clear to everyone.

And what is clear, after all—what the majority at any one pinpoint of myopic human history agrees on? Understand this: The journey to him and with him is one-by-one, not en masse. There is no Scripture, no story, no experience of him that cannot be gainsaid by the unbelieving. There must always be room for the personal discovery, the glory of hearing one's own name called.

EDWARDS: Finally, then, what one believes doesn't matter.

LEWIS: Are you even listening? God forbid! It matters, because at the end of self, to which all of us eventually come, awaits God. The path you take can be better or less lighted, can contain more or fewer obstacles, can be hastened or inhibited, can confuse or bless others on the journey.

EDWARDS: The end of self?

LEWIS: You know the story of the Prodigal! He couldn't make the journey home until he came to the end of himself, by which the Son meant the end of our claims on self. Forgive me, but let's say it bluntly: When we die, it is the end of our claims to use our and only our suspect lexicons and epistemologies to define ourselves, our neighbors, and the universe. We can choose to die now—die to self—or let death perform this function without our permission. A rather dreadful conclusion, mind you.

On Terra, Christianity alone ("mere" Christianity, I hasten to add) can truly represent this (if I
may say it) disarmingly wider view, a faith simultaneously affirming unique, significant personhood
while at the same time explaining how things went
awry and how God acted to put them aright. Cosmic
in import, compassionate in comport.

"Mere" Christianity is resilient, you know:
the regenerated life redeemed from the ravages
of sectarian, culture-hued, gender-striven, zeitgeist-
driven dogma. In a word, the life he lived, and
lives.

EDWARDS: Okay, so just where is this "mere" Christianity, Jack?

LEWIS: All over, everywhere—if you seek it you will
find it. (I created Narnia as a lamppost to illuminate
the way, you know!) But, mind you, it doesn't come
self-labeled. And it certainly isn't, in the worst sense
of that terran word, *popular*. It won't be on your six
o'clock news. It defies denominational possession and
captivity. Rather, it's a journey you must undertake
for yourself. But there are some marvelous comrades
along the way, I must say.

EDWARDS: Jack, I . . .

LEWIS: Must go, old fellow. Good chatting. Very
sorry I can't be helpful in the way you'd like. But even

if I could be, it would do you no good. You don't need my answers, you need yours, the ones God grants you. And you shall have them! All his answers are analogous to all others, but always in the language, the images, the colours in which you alone can see and hear them: "Come unto me ye heavy-laden and I will give you rest."

He comes to you, and you alone, in what he says to you and how he says it. The "rest" he promises to you—I couldn't begin to guess or articulate. That, thankfully, is his business. His only one, I might add . . .

EDWARDS: Jack, one more question . . .

LEWIS: Must take my leave, dear boy. More stories to hear. Tollers has written a real page-turner this time, if I may say so, and I must get a hot cup of tea . . . Cheers!

The conversation ended abruptly—an unexpected outage by the ISP perhaps? Jack was gone. *Was it Jack? Was it a dream? A vision?*

I stepped back from the computer screen, squinting, quivering in the light of paradox, chastened by the poverty of my own intellect, curiously warmed by the rediscovery of my mortality, and eager to find what truly lies beyond it.

As we sail on toward Aslan's country, I dream of home . . .

All their life in this world and their adventures in Narnia had only been the cover and the title page: now at last they were beginning Chapter One of the Great Story which no one on earth has read: which goes on forever: in which every chapter is better than the one before.[16]

THE LAST BATTLE

SUGGESTED READING

As I said in the Prologue, *Not a Tame Lion* is not intended to replace or duplicate the very sturdy work that has already been done on the Chronicles of Narnia. The texts I cite below have been helpful to me in recent years. Some are long out of print but are available through an interlibrary loan system.

Lewis discusses his motivations and the premises behind the Narnia tales in three essays: "On Three Ways of Writing for Children," "Sometimes Fairy Stories May Say Best What's to Be Said," and "It All Began with a Picture." These are collected in *On Stories* (ed. Walter Hooper, Harvest Books, 1982; 2002).

It is tempting to list a dozen or so of the many important single essays on the Chronicles, but my purpose here is to provide a short list of immediately accessible and helpful works, not a bibliography. I have recommended books that deal exclusively with the Narnia tales, with two exceptions. To me, these two are essential to understanding the development of Lewis's "baptized imagination." The following works deserve your attention and will enhance your appreciation and love of Narnia:

DAVID DOWNING

The Most Reluctant Convert (InterVarsity, 2002)

No contemporary Lewis scholar writes with more consistent poignancy and authority than David Downing. This work is the best treatment yet of Lewis's conversion and, thus, of the redemption of his imagination and the impact of his conversion on his postadolescent search for joy. This book is not focused on the Chronicles of Narnia, but readers will find here much food for thought about why Lewis became the writer—and the Christian—that he did. Professor Downing's richly illustrated intellectual and spiritual tapestry supports our reading of the Narnia stories.

COLIN DURIEZ

A Field Guide to Narnia (InterVarsity, 2004)

This work of Colin Duriez is only the latest in his signal contribution to our understanding of the Inklings' imaginative landscapes; by delightfully delineating Lewis's mythopoeia, he shows us why we are still reading the Chronicles and why we will continue to do so for the foreseeable future.

PAUL FORD

Companion to Narnia (HarperCollins, 1994)

Paul Ford's work is undoubtedly the most comprehensive and delightful of the handbooks on Narnia. It contains page after page of insight on the breadth and subtlety of the Narnia tales. No Narnia lover's library is complete without a copy of this extremely valuable Companion.

WALTER HOOPER
Past Watchful Dragons (Collier, 1979)
Because Walter Hooper is the most perspicacious of all
Lewis commentators, it is only right that his early work on
Narnia be counted first among the compact monographs on
the Chronicles. Much of *Dragons* has been updated and in-
corporated into Hooper's *C. S. Lewis: Companion and Guide*
(HarperCollins, 1996), but the original volume continues to
provide a useful, very personal account of Lewis's creative
faculties.

C. S. LEWIS
Boxen, ed. Walter Hooper (Harcourt, 1986)
This fascinating travelogue of Lewis's childhood imagination is replete with surviving stories and drawings from
the very precocious Jacksie. Though not exactly the proto-
type of Narnia's spiritual world, *Boxen*'s Animal-Land
has amazingly sophisticated, witty, and wise "dressed
animals," each on their own search for what is real and
meaningful.

KATHRYN LINDSKOOG
The Lion of Judah in Never-Never Land (Eerdmans, 1973)
and *Journey into Narnia* (Hope, 1998)
These two books by the late Kay Lindskoog are the first and
the best commentaries on why Narnia is so dear to us and
why Lewis continues to invite so many of us on the journey
of faith more than forty years after his death.

COLIN MANLOVE

The Chronicles of Narnia: The Patterning of a Fantastic World
(Twayne, 1993)
This book is an intellectually challenging yet readable treatment of the encompassing themes and unique narrative features of the Narnia Chronicles by a formidable and prolific fantasy and science-fiction scholar. Professor Manlove's volume is valuable in that he writes as a consummate literary critic, not as a fan. He appreciates the nuances of Lewis's style and his uncommon achievement in the tales.

PETER J. SCHAKEL

Imagination and the Arts in C. S. Lewis: Journeying to Narnia and Other Worlds (University of Missouri Press, 2002) and *Reading with the Heart* (Eerdmans, 1979)
Peter Schakel's two works on Narnia, like Kay Lindskoog's, give us historical perspective on our scholarly understanding and literary appreciation of the Chronicles. Published twenty-three years apart, Professor Schakel's volumes help us to understand Lewis's multilayered creative achievement and elucidate the influence of Lewis's prose on successive generations of readers.

STUDY GUIDE FOR

NOT A TAME LION

with chapter-by-chapter readings

C. S. Lewis understood our need to recognize and embrace the creativity of our Creator. From boyhood, he nurtured an appreciation for stories of other worlds, and through them was able to touch readers' hearts with God's hope. This study guide is an invitation to continue the journey to a world beyond our own.

You can use this study guide in a variety of ways. You might begin with the first question and follow on through to the end; or choose only those questions that pertain to your current circumstances; or focus on the questions that apply to a particular book in the Chronicles of Narnia.

To enhance your study, we have included a list of suggested readings in the Chronicles that will guide you to specific chapters and help you find the readings and allusions discussed in *Not a Tame Lion*.

We have used the following abbreviations for the Narnian tales:

LWW: *The Lion, the Witch, and the Wardrobe*
PC: *Prince Caspian*
VDT: *The Voyage of the "Dawn Treader"*
SC: *The Silver Chair*
HB: *The Horse and His Boy*
MN: *The Magician's Nephew*
LB: *The Last Battle*

CHAPTER 1–INKLINGS OF NEVERLAND: C. S. LEWIS AND THE ORIGINS OF NARNIA

OUT OF THE SHADOW-LANDS (PAGE 4)

1. C. S. Lewis's childhood loss of his mother and his traumatic early years in the academic world led to great cynicism that distanced him from a relationship with God. Spend a few moments reviewing your life experiences. How have they affected your current spiritual state and your views of and feelings about God?

2. In *The Problem of Pain*, "Lewis endeavored to reconcile the concept of a good, all-powerful God with the presence of evil and suffering in the universe he had created." With this statement, Edwards broaches one of life's most confusing conundrums: How could God allow such pain and evil in the world? How would you answer that question?

3. C. S. Lewis wrestled with questions about God's existence, his involvement and care in our lives, and his goodness. Most of us have faced similar struggles on some level. When have you faced doubts or fears about God's identity, character, and role in your life? Read Deuteronomy 31:8, Psalm 37:28, and Matthew 6:25-34. What hope do the promises in these Scriptures offer?

4. Edwards states that Lewis wrote about the essentials of the Christian faith—what unites us instead of divides us. What are some divisions you see among Christian denominations? Which, if any, are driven by essential doctrines, and which are of lesser importance, based on differing interpretations of the Bible?

SURPRISED BY ASLAN (PAGE 11)

1. Close on the heels of the publication of the Narnia series came Lewis's spiritual autobiography, *Surprised by Joy*. If you could sum up in one word or phrase your own spiritual autobiography, what would it be? What themes or lessons do you hope or think will be addressed in the remainder of your story of faith?

2. What were the major influences (people, places, circumstances, successes, failures) that shaped your early life and your faith? What do you observe about the effects of those influences in your adult life?

3. Define *joy* in your own words. Have you ever felt surprised by joy? How do you think a person finds true joy?

4. How can the "notions that the past is invariably wrong

and that the present is always the barometer of truth" hinder a person from finding God?

RE-ENCHANTMENT AND IMAGINATION (PAGE 25)

1. Consider for a moment what the universe might be like if God did not have an imagination. Next, consider what it would be like if God had created the cosmos without using reason. Describe your thoughts about both.

2. Explain what Edwards means by the following statement: "Imagination is the counterpart and complement to reason." What roles do imagination and reason play in helping a person understand and live in the world?

3. What roles do imagination and reason play in a person's faith in Christ? (See Ephesians 1:18-19.)

4. Edwards describes Jesus as the Son of God; a Shepherd; the King of kings; the Morning Star; the Way, the Truth, and the Life; a Lamb; and a Lion. Briefly describe the characteristics each one embodies.

NOT A TAME AUTHOR (PAGE 28)

1. Review the Creation story in Genesis 1:1–2:14. Briefly describe your observations about God's artistic nature shown in his creative work.

2. Edwards discusses the "true myth" of the biblical story of the universe and humanity. Why is it important to our identity and place in the world to understand where we came from and the ultimate potential of our future hope?

3. The world as we see it "is withstood and understood only by those with an unfathomably wild anticipation of a soon, sure redemption." Where in your life do you struggle? What brings you hope during tough times?

4. Describe various ways you observe society's loss of imagination and belief in a world beyond our own. How would day-to-day life on earth be different if everyone truly believed in and lived for the hope of heaven?

CHAPTER 2–ENCOUNTERING ASLAN: *THE DANGER OF GOODNESS*

THE COST OF GOODNESS (PAGE 40)

Suggested readings:

- *The Pevensie children's first conversation about Aslan with Mr. Beaver, in* LWW, *chapter 7.*
- *Mr. Beaver's description of Aslan, in* LWW, *chapter 8.*
- *The Pevensie children's first direct encounter with Aslan, in* LWW, *chapter 12.*
- *The children's memory of Mr. Beaver's comments about Aslan "not being a tame lion," in* LWW, *chapter 17.*
- *Jadis, the destroyer of Charn and evil Queen of Narnia, is introduced, in* MN, *chapter 5.*

1. Define goodness in your own words.

2. Describe what Edwards means by the following statement: "Goodness is fierce and furious, formidable and aggressive, shocking and dangerous." Is this insight new for you? How do you reconcile this powerful view

of goodness with the fruit of the Spirit described in Galatians 5:22-23?

3. Goodness is often viewed as one-dimensional or simplistic. Good characters are often seen as boring or superficial. How do Lewis's and Edwards's thoughts about this topic bring freshness and depth to the word *good?*

4. Relate Edwards's discussion of goodness to what the Bible says in Matthew 10:16. Consider and expand on what life would be like if our formidable, aggressive, dangerous God were not also good.

MEETING ASLAN IN *THE LION, THE WITCH, AND THE WARDROBE* (PAGE 45)

Suggested readings:

- *Mr. Beaver's description of Aslan, in* LWW, *chapter 8.*
- *The Pevensie children's first direct encounter with Aslan, in* LWW, *chapter 12.*

1. "When the Pevensie children first hear Aslan's name, they have an intuitive sense of what it means . . . that Aslan is on the move." What is *your* intuitive response to the news that "Aslan is on the move"? How is "Aslan" on the move in our day and age?

2. Edwards writes, "Yes, this is the ideal way to meet Aslan— as Lewis did and as Peter, Susan, and Lucy do. He is good and terrible, with his flash of golden mane, his deep and penetrating eyes. His name, his mane, and his manner command awe, reverence, and obedience. We see him in a close and personal way." How does encountering Jesus

in the character of Aslan affect your understanding of him? Have you ever thought of Jesus as "good and terrible"? Explain.

THE SINGING CREATOR IN *THE MAGICIAN'S NEPHEW* (PAGE 51)

Suggested readings:

- *Aslan sings Narnia into existence, in* MN, *chapter 9.*
- *Digory resists the temptation of the Queen and obeys Aslan; and the Witch is defeated, in* MN, *chapters 13 and 14.*

1. Edwards discusses varying sides of Aslan's nature. In *The Lion, the Witch, and the Wardrobe*, Lewis presents Aslan "up close" in relating to the characters, and the great Lion plays the role of Savior. In *The Magician's Nephew*, Aslan's creative, artistic nature comes to the fore. Consider God's nature as Creator. What does his creation reveal about his character?

2. Edwards describes several of Aslan's actions that show the Lion's sovereign and gracious rule over his subjects. Draw some parallels between these actions and God's sovereignty throughout history.

3. "Seemingly innocent actions can have powerful consequences." Give an example from your own life (or from something you've observed) that illustrates Edwards's statement.

4. Edwards discusses parallels between the characters of the Narnia books and the story of humanity—mistakes and all. What are some real-life historical events that

demonstrate how people have consistently desired to "find fulfillment, lasting happiness, and peace apart from God"?

CHAPTER 3–VALOR FINDS VALIDATION: *REIGNING WITH ASLAN*

THE PEVENSIES IN *THE LION, THE WITCH, AND THE WARDROBE* (PAGE 62)

Suggested readings:

- *Edmund expresses mistrust of fauns, in* LWW, *chapter 4.*
- *Professor Kirke defends Lucy's trustworthiness, in* LWW, *chapter 5.*
- *Mr. Beaver rebukes Edmund's skepticism about Aslan, in* LWW, *chapter 8.*
- *Eustace and Edmund discuss Aslan's loving character, in* VDT, *chapter 7.*

1. Edwards states that "openness to wonder is a necessary component for thriving in Aslan's kingdom." What role does wonder play in faith?
2. Consider this statement: "When the rumors begin that Aslan is on the move, true Narnians are exhilarated, whereas faithless ones are alarmed." Explain Edwards's comment that "cowardice breeds contempt for the holy and the true." How could a lack of reverence for holiness reveal cowardice? How is this evident in the world today?
3. Review the "trilemma" that Professor Kirke poses to the children regarding Lucy's claim about having visited

Narnia. How does the "must be" forced by a trilemma challenge someone to valorous action instead of mere speculation?

4. Consider the gift of a second chance, first as we see it in Edmund's life, and then as we can experience it through Christ's death. When asked if he knows Aslan, Edmund responds, "Well, he knows me." Edwards comments that "to know as we are known is the great promise of heaven and of dwelling in Narnia. Once upon a time, Edmund did not know the cost paid by the Lion for his life. Now he does. . . . Redeemed and rectified, Edmund is now in a position to train others in the grace and mercy of Aslan." How does Edmund's growth in the virtue of valor parallel the life of a Christian?

PRINCE CASPIAN IN *PRINCE CASPIAN* (PAGE 68)

Suggested readings:

- *The Pevensies learn of what has happened to Narnia, and Dr. Cornelius is presented as a wise mentor to Caspian, in* PC, *chapter 4.*
- *The ancient stories of Narnia are recalled and used to guide the plan to save Narnia in the present, in* PC, *chapter 7.*

1. Consider this excerpt from chapter 3: "Narnian society, set right by Aslan's earlier sacrifice and resurrection, seems to have developed a cultural and historical amnesia, and a dark age has set in. How could this be? What has gone wrong? Narnia's development has been

225

arrested, and painful and debilitating questions have arisen. What should one believe? Why should anyone believe in the old stories? Does Aslan even exist?" In what ways does this reflection resemble what often happens to faith traditions in real-life society?

2. Expand on Edwards's claim that "one's vantage point is crucial and that one is responsible for both what and how one sees" regarding valorous actions and holding to truth over time.

3. Just as Caspian must surround himself with "trustworthy, like-minded folk who also believe"—the fearless Trumpkin and the valiant Reepicheep—how is our valor tested and refined, or possibly weakened, by the companions we choose?

4. Explain the relationship between coming to terms with personal weaknesses and valor based on the following statement: "'If you had felt yourself sufficient, it would have been a proof that you were not.' Caspian needed to know the limits of his own powers, and when to rely on others—especially Aslan—to win the day."

JILL POLE IN *THE SILVER CHAIR* (PAGE 74)
Suggested readings:
- *Jill and Eustace escape from Bullies into Narnia, in* SC, *chapter 1.*
- *Jill meets Aslan for the first time, in* SC, *chapter 2.*

1. The role of wonder in faith emerges again in *The Silver Chair*, when Eustace asks Jill if she is good at believing

in things that others would laugh at. Jill responds that she thinks she would be if given the chance. How is our intellect related to faith? How does it either help or hinder our faith?

2. Explain and expand on Edwards's comment that "relationships are built on experiential, not experimental, knowledge."

3. People of faith are sometimes viewed as weak, needing a crutch to survive life. However, Edwards claims that "courage is another quality necessary for faith." Describe a situation in which faith requires courage.

4. Edwards quotes Aslan saying to Jill, "You would not have called to me unless I had been calling to you." Have you ever felt God calling you to a new goal or to a closer relationship with him? Explain the circumstances and your response. How was your character challenged or changed?

PUDDLEGLUM IN *THE SILVER CHAIR* (PAGE 80)
Suggested readings:

- *Puddleglum asserts his faith in Aslan, not "accidents," in SC, chapter 10.*
- *Puddleglum rises to the occasion and defeats the Queen by his courage and his commitment to Aslan, in SC, chapter 12.*

1. Puddleglum is not a particularly charismatic character. In fact, he typically can't see the silver lining in the cloud. Nevertheless, he is loyal to the end, both to the

truth and to Providence. Expand on how the character trait of loyalty shows valor. Do you know anyone like Puddleglum?

2. Do you believe in *accidents* or *coincidences?* Why or why not? What biblical support do you have for your view?

3. Edwards writes, "The steadfast Puddleglum, under torture, declares that he will believe in Narnia and live as a Narnian—even if he has only dreamed that there is such a place as Narnia and such a lion as Aslan." Expand on how faith sometimes looks foolish in the eyes of the faithless. Which do you think is the greater loss, being seen as a fool for maintaining steadfast faith that is proven wrong, or seeing someone as a fool for having that faith? Explain.

4. One theme of *The Silver Chair* is that things are not always as they appear, whether it is people or circumstances. How can confusion weaken valor?

DIGORY KIRKE AND POLLY PLUMMER IN *THE MAGICIAN'S NEPHEW* (PAGE 84)

Suggested readings:

- *We learn why Digory finds himself in the care of the Ketterleys, in* MN, *chapter 1.*
- *Uncle Andrew is introduced as vain and deceitful, in* MN, *chapter 2.*
- *Digory awakens Jadis, in* MN, *chapter 4.*
- *Digory and Polly hear the awful story of Charn's destruction, in* MN, *chapter 5.*

- *Digory and Polly witness the birth of Narnia, in* MN, *chapter 9.*
- *Digory resists Jadis's treachery and returns the Apple to Aslan, in* MN, *chapter 13.*
- *The origins of the Wardrobe are revealed, in* MN, *chapter 14.*
- *Digory's mother is saved, in* MN, *chapter 15.*

1. Edwards states that "personal trials and losses can derail one's faith and hope," an insight he develops based on the losses many characters face throughout the Narnia series. Has your faith ever been threatened by a personal struggle? Have you witnessed someone else's faith falter due to difficult times? What Scripture verses offer hope and strength during times of trouble? (Feel free to use a concordance for assistance.)

2. Digory chooses to submit to Aslan's authority despite his belief that his choice will mean his mother's death. Submission is often viewed as taking the role of follower instead of leader. However, how can submission reveal courage and valor? What is the difference between assertive submission and passive submission?

3. How does refusing to submit to authority result in an inability to know the truth or hear God's leading?

4. Edwards closes this section with an interesting statement about two kinds of Narnians. What are they? Draw the parallel between the theology of Narnia and Christian

theology. What will be the differing results of assertive submission and passive submission to God during the end times?

CHAPTER 4–VICTORY OVER VANITY: TRANSFORMATIONS AND REVIVALS

EUSTACE, CASPIAN, AND LUCY IN *THE VOYAGE OF THE "DAWN TREADER"* (PAGE 93)

Suggested readings:

- *Eustace is introduced as a selfish and pretentious young man, in* VDT, *chapter 1.*
- *Eustace and Reepicheep trade insults, in* VDT, *chapter 2.*
- *Eustace becomes a dragon and is rescued by Aslan, in* VDT, *chapter 6.*
- *Lucy battles against vanity and pride and is confronted by Aslan, in* VDT, *chapter 10.*
- *Prince Caspian tries to abdicate and sail with Reepicheep; Lucy and Edmund learn they are not to return to Narnia, in* VDT, *chapter 16.*

1. Expand on Edwards's statement that "vanity is at the heart of every betrayal, lie, seizure of power, and act of vengeance or treachery." In what ways have you sensed vanity at work in your thoughts, attitudes, and actions? What do you think about the claim that vanity is a sign or result of a competitive nature?

2. Edwards connects the sin of pride with a lack of imagination. How are the two related, and how does

imagination counteract pride? What do you think of his statement that "imagination is seeing with the heart, seeing oneself in true relationship to the universe one inhabits"?

3. How is seeing ourselves as either better or worse than we actually are a sign of vanity? How does a personal encounter with God clear up who we are in his eyes? How is your self-perception or self-image in agreement or conflict with how God sees you? How is your self-image helping or hindering your relationship with the Lord and with others?

4. Explain how the following statement relates to vanity's influence: "The persistent pursuit of anything short of absolute joy leads to ruin and sentences the soul to jealousy and despair." (You may need to take another look at the text to review how Edwards builds his argument.) Consider the destructive effects of vanity on our ability to experience true joy.

SHASTA AND ARAVIS IN *THE HORSE AND HIS BOY* (PAGE 103)

Suggested readings:

- *The history of Calormen; Shasta's encounter with Bree, the talking horse, in* HB, *chapter 1.*
- *Aravis and Hwin explain their trek to Shasta and Bree, in* HB, *chapter 3.*
- *Aravis asserts her nobility and superior attitudes, in* HB, *chapter 4.*

- *Bree sarcastically rebukes Hwin, in* HB, *chapter 9.*
- *Shasta, Aravis, Bree, and Hwin encounter the wise Hermit, in* HB, *chapter 10.*
- *Shasta meets Aslan, in* HB, *chapter 11.*
- *Aslan mercifully but firmly confronts Bree and Aravis and tenderly welcomes Hwin, in* HB, *chapter 14.*

1. Consider the following statement: "Only by being in the midst of unfamiliar territory with its geographical, cultural, and emotional contrasts can we fully understand ourselves or others. Lewis wants us to see Narnia afresh, but indirectly, through the eyes of Shasta and Aravis as they emerge from their bondage in Calormen. What a culture believes determines how its citizens treat one another, and the deity they worship creates them in his image." Consider various foreign cultures and religions that differ from yours. What observations can you make about the societal effects of religious beliefs and faith? What is each individual's responsibility, if any, to understand and tolerate other cultures and religions? In what ways are you challenged by those responsibilities?

2. Read Exodus 20:3, Psalm 34:14, 1 Timothy 2:2, James 3:17, and 1 Peter 3:11. How do the truths expressed in these verses work together when it comes to tolerance of other religions and staying true to the first commandment that there is only one God?

3. This section contains beautiful discussions of the work of Providence and seeking our true home. Do any

quotes stand out particularly to you? Write them down and place them where you can see them each day. How have you seen Providence at work in your own life or the lives of others? Do you relate to a feeling of restlessness for something beyond this life on earth? If so, what circumstances trigger that longing?

4. How can our lives be "stifled by [our] own smugness and snobbishness," as Edwards describes Aravis's life? Have you ever been given a taste of your own medicine? How did the lesson affect your character and future behavior?

CHAPTER 5–VILLAINY MEETS VICIOUSNESS: WITCHES, TRAITORS, AND BETRAYERS

JADIS, QUEEN OF NARNIA, IN *THE MAGICIAN'S NEPHEW* AND THE WHITE WITCH IN *THE LION, THE WITCH, AND THE WARDROBE* (PAGE 122)

Suggested readings:

- *Edmund encounters the White Witch, in* LWW, *chapter 4.*
- *The White Witch's lair is revealed, as well as her treacherous plans, in* LWW, *chapter 9.*
- *The White Witch's reaction to Aslan's name; the threat of the coming thaw, in* LWW, *chapter 11.*
- *The White Witch and Aslan debate the meaning of the Deep Magic, in* LWW, *chapter 13.*
- *Aslan is killed and the White Witch exults in her apparent victory, in* LWW, *chapter 14.*

- *Aslan triumphs and the White Witch is overcome, in* LWW, *chapter 15.*
- *Digory awakens Jadis, in* MN, *chapter 4.*
- *Jadis narrates the destruction of Charn gleefully, in* MN, *chapter 5.*
- *Digory resists Jadis's treachery and returns the Apple to Aslan, in* MN, *chapter 13.*
- *Jadis's demise is explained, in* MN, *chapter 14.*

1. Explain the following statement: "Evil is monotonous, unimaginative, predictable, flat, and colorless. . . . There is but one way to be evil: to 'be oneself' to the nth degree."

2. Discuss how Edwards contrasts evil with his comments about goodness: "By contrast, good is diverse, multihued, fascinating, and enduring. There are many ways to be good, because goodness is infinite in its manifestations."

3. There is strength in goodness and weakness in evil. Consider Edwards's comments about how Edmund's envy and jealousy lead to his being easily duped by the witch. Many people seem to think that God's call for us to be obedient to his ways is simply for goodness' sake. However, in what ways does goodness strengthen us for battling temptations and for protecting ourselves and others against the evils in the world? How does ignoring God's ways weaken us?

4. "All get what they want, but they do not always like it.

[Jadis's] fate is that of all who desire to be immortally 'themselves.'" In what ways is "mere self-survival . . . a less than ultimate good"?

UNCLE ANDREW IN *THE MAGICIAN'S NEPHEW* (PAGE 136)

Suggested readings:

- *Uncle Andrew is introduced as vain and deceitful, in* MN, *chapter 2.*
- *Jadis and Uncle Andrew are dismayed by Aslan's creation song, in* MN, *chapter 9.*
- *Aslan warns Digory and Polly of future trouble in their world, in* MN, *chapter 15.*

1. Based on Edwards's discussion of evil as seen in Uncle Andrew, describe in your own words how evil is cowardly.

2. Do you ever find yourself craving control or power over others? What effects on your spirit do those cravings create? Peace? Patience?

3. Why is it difficult to accept the authority of others? Describe the difference between wanting some say in your situation and wanting to control your situation. At what point does a desire for control become detrimental?

4. We all struggle with selfishness because human nature is selfish. What lessons have you learned in life regarding your own selfishness? How have you grown toward being unselfish?

THE QUEEN OF THE UNDERLAND IN *THE SILVER CHAIR* (PAGE 139)

Suggested reading:

- *The Queen's lies and treachery are defeated by the courage of Puddleglum, in* SC, *chapter 12.*

1. What is the importance of truth as a protector against evil?
2. When have you experienced evil's subtlety in drawing you away from God's truth?
3. What are some of Satan's most pervasive lies that are believed by society today? Identify a couple of scriptural truths that combat those lies.
4. How does Satan use confusion as a way of muddling the truth and weakening our resolve to obey God?

NIKABRIK IN *PRINCE CASPIAN* (PAGE 143)

Suggested readings:

- *Nikabrik is introduced and his faithlessness is revealed, in* PC, *chapter 6.*
- *Nikabrik's cynicism leads him into bad company and, eventually, to death, in* PC, *chapter 12.*

1. Edwards discusses the world-weariness of Nikabrik the dwarf and how that makes him susceptible to believing anything. Share your thoughts on how the destructive character trait of cynicism has a snowballing effect.
2. "The tale of Nikabrik . . . is Lewis's cautionary tale to any civilization inebriated by self-importance and the

NOT A TAME LION

supposed ability to thrive without historical perspective or relationship with God. This is chronological snobbery gone wild, a disposition to disbelieve the old stories and to substitute a contrary meaning for the original." What role does Christian history play in establishing and protecting us against evil?

3. "To divorce oneself from this ["grand narrative"], from the true character of Aslan and the real adventures of his loyal subjects, is to sentence oneself to disenchantment, self-doubt, and despair." Our culture often values "progressiveness" over "old-fashioned" views, beliefs, and behaviors. What are some truly positive examples of progressiveness that we enjoy, and what are some old traditions and beliefs that we need to preserve?

4. How can a lack of respect and adherence to historical beliefs be as destructive as "sheer violence and physical intimidation"? What practical things can Christians do to resist the force of cultural ways that "mock our [views of heaven] and undermine the promise of our citizenship there"?

CHAPTER 6–VINDICATION AND VALEDICTION: LAST BATTLES, LAST WORDS

NOT A TAME LION REVISITED (PAGE 158)

Suggested readings:

- *Shift sets up his deception, in* LB, *chapter 1.*
- *King Tirian and Jewel come to grips with the apparent return of Aslan, in* LB, *chapter 2.*

237

1. Do you ever find yourself preoccupied with "next things"—all the items remaining on your never-ending to-do list? What are you waiting for at the end of your life on earth? Do those hopes supply patience to your life here and now, or do they bring anxiety? Explain.

2. How does believing that this life is all there is or failing to focus on the life to come lead to despair or cynicism?

3. Much of Edwards's discussion in this section revolves around Aslan's sovereignty and how many Narnian characters struggle to understand his ways. When has a certain aspect of God's character or his ways been difficult for you to grasp or accept? Have you found clarity for your questions? If so, how did it come about?

4. Why do so many people resist believing in the one true God? What may seem unappealing about him? What seems appealing about other faiths?

TASH VS. ASLAN IN *THE LAST BATTLE* (PAGE 162)

Suggested readings:

- *Shift and Ginger spin their web of lies about Aslan, in* LB, *chapter 3.*
- *Tirian calls upon Aslan for rescue, in* LB, *chapter 4.*
- *Aslan answers the call for help by sending Jill and Eustace back to Narnia, in* LB, *chapter 5.*
- *The faithlessness of the dwarfs is explored, in* LB, *chapter 7.*
- *The end of Narnia draws closer, in* LB, *chapter 8.*

1. Many Narnian characters lost faith in Aslan because of fear prompted by lies told by Shift, the Ape. Fear is one of Satan's most powerful weapons in his arsenal against God and us. What do you fear? What scriptural truths alleviate those fears and bolster your confidence in God?

2. Disappointment, weariness, and disillusionment with life weakened the Narnians' resolve to hold fast to their belief in Aslan and opened their minds to being duped into submission to the pagan god Tash. What are some ways to combat the arrows that life throws at you and remain firm in your faith?

3. Not only were the citizens of Narnia lacking discernment to know that they were being tricked, but they also lost their historical faith in what they had known of Aslan's character. Thus, the lines between Tash and Aslan were muddied in their minds, and the false god "Tashlan" became a real being to them. In what ways does our society muddy the distinction between truth and error?

4. Edwards shares an interesting insight about the difference between Tash and Aslan, which parallels the difference between Satan and God: "Tash, 'the inexorable, the irresistible,' is not Aslan's equal in any way, any more than Satan is God's counterpart in some dualistic universe." How does the knowledge that Satan is not all-powerful affect your life?

SUSAN AND EMETH IN *THE LAST BATTLE* (PAGE 169)

Suggested readings:

- *Emeth demands to go into the Stable to meet Tash, in* LB, *chapter 10.*
- *Tash is vanquished; the truth is revealed; Susan is missed, in* LB, *chapter 12.*
- *A grand reunion and the story of Emeth's redemption, in* LB, *chapter 15.*

1. "One must guard one's heart vigilantly on either side of the Wardrobe." What does it mean to guard one's heart, and how is it accomplished amid the demands, busyness, and conflicting appeals of daily life? What are potential consequences of not guarding one's heart?

2. Although Emeth believes he is serving Tash diligently, it is impossible to serve something so evil with true valor, noble intentions, and purity of heart. Therefore, Aslan welcomes Emeth and tells him he has been worshiping Aslan all along, because Emeth's heart has always been noble and pure. He says, "It is better to see the Lion and die than to be Tisroc of the world and live and not to have seen him." What might Lewis be saying about how Aslan's response parallels God's grace? What might he say about the importance of the condition of our hearts?

3. Discuss Edwards's definition of grace and mercy: "Grace is getting credit for things one didn't do; mercy is not receiving blame for the things one has done."

4. Do you ever struggle to accept God's grace in your life? Is God's grace sometimes difficult to understand? Explain.

FAREWELL TO SHADOW-LANDS (PAGE 171)
Suggested reading:
* *The new Narnia beckons, in* LB, *chapter 16.*

1. Take another look at your definition of joy from the study questions for chapter 1. What is the quality of joy in your life these days? What threatens your joy? What proactive measure are you taking to protect it?

2. Expand on Edwards's claim that "the seeker must not put [joy] first, or he will miss both joy and its byproducts—happiness, peace, and contentment shared in a community of comrades."

3. Explain how a biblical view of history—having an end in two senses, a termination point and a purpose—conflicts with the cyclical view (recycling or reincarnation) that many people hold. What is the importance of having a purpose in life? What are some effects of losing a sense of purpose? What effects might evil have if it were allowed to go on indefinitely and if God did not intend to destroy it forever?

4. How do you feel about your own mortality? Does the reality of death make you feel anxious? Fearful? Hopeful? Peaceful? Joyful? How do you think God wants you to feel?

EPILOGUE–AFTER NARNIA

RE-ENCHANTING OUR COSMOS (PAGE 179)

Suggested readings:

- *Professor Kirke defends Lucy and explains why she can be trusted, in* LWW, *chapter 5.*
- *Ramandu instructs Eustace in "seeing with the heart," in* VDT, *chapter 14.*

1. "Lewis could anchor his vocation, his faith, and his life in something other than newspaper headlines or the vagaries of modern science." In what or in whom is your life anchored?

2. Edwards says that we must cultivate a "disciplined imagination." What do you think he means by this? What does an undisciplined imagination look like?

3. What do you see as some of the dangers of "reducing the imagination to wishful thinking" when it comes to trusting God and preparing for life after death?

4. Consider this statement: "With neither heaven nor science to guide us, we elect 'whatever' to give shape to our lives, even if it is the mirage that we can make up our story as we go along: my world and welcome to it. My story doesn't have to connect to anything; I will live it out, one day at a time, without regard to its having ultimate purpose, because any value it has is only what I invest it with."

5. Summarize in your own words the differences between what Edwards refers to as "looking along" and "looking

at." What are the strengths and weaknesses of both, and why must they work together instead of one superseding the other? (Consider his discussion of reducing claims of truth to personal opinion.)

NARNIAN APOLOGETICS (PAGE 188)

1. Explain the idea that "all that is not eternal is eternally out of date." How does this compare with many worldviews today?
2. Read 1 Peter 3:15. How ready are you to share about your spiritual beliefs? What is the value of being prepared to share your faith?
3. Edwards claims that C. S. Lewis's effectiveness in sharing his faith lies in the fact that he knew what it was like to be lost. What is the value of remembering where we've come from and what God has saved us from?
4. What is the importance of the intellect, a broken and restored heart, and an unfailing empathy for the lost in a balanced and effective faith?

LEWIS REDUX (PAGE 196)

1. What are some highlights of *Not a Tame Lion* that stood out to you?
2. What questions do you still have regarding any of the themes in The Chronicles of Narnia or *Not a Tame Lion?*
3. List any views you have that differ from the ones presented in the book.

243

4. Where do you go from here? How will your life be
   changed through the insights and observations you've
   made on your journey through *Not a Tame Lion?*

NOTES

ACKNOWLEDGMENTS
1. C. S. Lewis, "The Weight of Glory," in *The Weight of Glory and Other Addresses* (Grand Rapids: Eerdmans, 1965), 5.

PROLOGUE
1. C. S. Lewis, *The Lion, the Witch, and the Wardrobe: A Story for Children* (New York: Macmillan, 1950), 149.
2. C. S. Lewis, *Studies in Medieval and Renaissance Literature,* comp. by Walter Hooper (Cambridge: Cambridge University Press, 1966), 4.
3. Ibid.
4. C. S. Lewis, *The Discarded Image* (Cambridge: Cambridge University Press, 1966), vii.

CHAPTER 1: INKLINGS OF NEVERLAND
1. C. S. Lewis, "On Three Ways of Writing for Children," in *On Stories, and Other Essays on Literature* (New York: Harcourt Brace Jovanovich, 1966), 25.
2. Ibid., 47.
3. Readers interested in a masterful account of Lewis's BBC performances and the response of the public should consult Justin Phillips, *C. S. Lewis at the BBC* (London: Marshall Pickering, 2003).
4. Bruce L. Edwards, ed., *The Taste of the Pineapple: Essays on C. S. Lewis as Reader, Critic, and Imaginative Writer* (Bowling Green, Ohio: Popular Press, 1988), 2.
5. C. S. Lewis, *Surprised by Joy: The Shape of My Early Life* (New York: Harcourt Brace & World, 1955), 20.
6. Ibid., viii.
7. Ibid., 237.

8. W. H. Lewis, ed., *Letters of C. S. Lewis* (New York: Harcourt Brace Jovanovich, 1975), 45.

9. Walter Hooper, "Preface," in Kathryn Lindskoog, *The Lion of Judah in Never-Never Land* (Grand Rapids: Eerdmans, 1973), 7.

10. C. S. Lewis, "The Weight of Glory," in *The Weight of Glory and Other Addresses* (Grand Rapids: Eerdmans, 1965), 5.

11. Lewis, *Surprised by Joy*, 191.

12. Ibid., 135.

13. Ibid., 137.

14. Ibid., 207.

15. For greater coverage of the Lewis-Tolkien friendship, see Colin Duriez, *Tolkien and C. S. Lewis: The Gift of Friendship* (Mahwah, N.J.: HiddenSpring, 2003).

16. C. S. Lewis, "Myth Become Fact," in *God in the Dock*, ed. Walter Hooper (Grand Rapids: Eerdmans, 1970), 66–67.

17. Lewis, *Surprised by Joy*, 228–229.

18. C. S. Lewis, *The Silver Chair* (New York: Macmillan, 1953), 17.

19. Humphrey Carpenter, *Tolkien: A Biography* (New York: Ballentine, 1977), 190.

20. Lewis, "Myth Become Fact," 66–67.

21. C. S. Lewis, *Mere Christianity* (New York: Macmillan, first paperback edition, 1960), 120.

22. C. S. Lewis, "Review of *The Hobbit*," in *On Stories, and Other Essays on Literature*, ed.Walter Hooper (New York: Harcourt Brace Jovanovich, 1982), 81.

23. C. S. Lewis, "Review of *The Lord of the Rings*," in *On Stories, and Other Essays on Literature*, ed. Walter Hooper (New York: Harcourt Brace Jovanovich, 1982), 89–90.

24. Lewis, "Weight of Glory," 5.

CHAPTER 2: ENCOUNTERING ASLAN

1. C. S. Lewis, *The Lion, the Witch, and the Wardrobe: A Story for Children* (New York: Macmillan, 1950), 64.

2. Ibid.

3. Roger Ebert, from his review of the movie *Hotel Rwanda*, published in the *Chicago Sun-Times*, December 22, 2004. The review can be found online at http://rogerebert.suntimes.com/apps/pbcs.dll/article?AID=/20041221/REVIEWS/41213001/1023.

4. C. S. Lewis, "It All Began with a Picture," in *On Stories and Other Essays on Literature*, ed. Walter Hooper (New York: Harcourt Brace Jovanovich, 1982), 52.

5. Lyle W. Dorsett and Marjorie Lamp Mead, eds., C. S. Lewis: *Letters to Children* (New York: Macmillan, 1985), 29.

6. Lewis, *The Lion, the Witch, and the Wardrobe*, 54–55.

7. Ibid., 63.

8. Dorsett and Mead, *Letters to Children*, 68–69.

9. Lewis, *The Lion, the Witch, and the Wardrobe*, 103.

10. Ibid., 104–105.

11. C. S. Lewis, *The Magician's Nephew* (New York: Macmillan, 1955), 87–88.

12. Ibid., 103

13. Ibid.

14. C. S. Lewis, "The Weight of Glory," in *The Weight of Glory and Other Addresses* (Grand Rapids: Eerdmans, 1965), 5.

15. Lewis, *The Lion, the Witch, and the Wardrobe*, 40.

16. C. S. Lewis, *Mere Christianity* (New York: Macmillan, first paperback edition, 1960), 53–54.

17. C. S. Lewis, "The World's Last Night," in *The World's Last Night and Other Essays* (New York: Harcourt Brace, 1960). This essay was first published in 1952 as "The Christian Hope—Its Meaning for Today."

CHAPTER 3: VALOR FINDS VALIDATION

1. C. S. Lewis, *The Voyage of the "Dawn Treader"* (New York: Macmillan, 1952), 91.

2. C. S. Lewis, *The Lion, the Witch, and the Wardrobe: A Story for Children* (New York: Macmillan, 1950), 38–39.

3. C. S. Lewis, *Mere Christianity* (New York: Macmillan, first paperback edition, 1960), 55–56.

4. Lewis, *The Lion, the Witch, and the Wardrobe*, 40.

5. Ibid., 33.

6. Ibid., 63–64.

7. Ibid.

8. Ibid., 133.

9. Ibid., 148.

10. Lewis, *Voyage of the "Dawn Treader,"* 91.

11. Letter from C. S. Lewis to Geoffrey Bles, 9-17-52 (Wade Center Collection).

12. C. S. Lewis, *Prince Caspian: The Return to Narnia* (New York: Macmillan, 1952), 41–42.
13. Ibid., 173.
14. C. S. Lewis, *The Silver Chair* (New York: Macmillan, 1953), 4.
15. Ibid., 7.
16. Ibid., 17.
17. Ibid., 19.
18. Ibid., 21.
19. Ibid., 154.
20. Ibid., 155.
21. Ibid., 131.
22. C. S. Lewis, *The Magician's Nephew* (New York: Macmillan, 1955), 153.

CHAPTER 4: VICTORY OVER VANITY

1. C. S. Lewis, *The Voyage of the "Dawn Treader"* (New York: Macmillan, 1952), 132.
2. C. S. Lewis, *Mere Christianity* (New York: Macmillan, first paperback edition, 1960), 109–110.
3. C. S. Lewis, *A Preface to Paradise Lost* (London: Oxford University Press, 1942), 102.
4. Lewis, *Voyage of the "Dawn Treader,"* 1.
5. Ibid.
6. Ibid., 4–5.
7. Ibid., 201.
8. Ibid., 202.
9. C. S. Lewis, "First and Second Things," in *God in the Dock*, ed. Walter Hooper (Grand Rapids: Eerdmans, 1970), 278–281.
10. Lewis, *Mere Christianity*, 118.
11. Lewis, *Voyage of the "Dawn Treader,"* 129.
12. Ibid., 132.
13. Ibid., 132–133.
14. Ibid., 208–209.
15. Ibid., 209.
16. C. S. Lewis, *The Lion, the Witch, and the Wardrobe: A Story for Children* (New York: Macmillan, 1950), 149.
17. C. S. Lewis, *The Horse and His Boy* (New York: Macmillan, 1954), 101.
18. Ibid., 2.
19. Ibid., 11.

20. C. S. Lewis, *Surprised by Joy: The Shape of My Early Life* (New York: Harcourt Brace & World, 1955), 73.
21. C. S. Lewis, "The Weight of Glory," in *The Weight of Glory and Other Addresses* (Grand Rapids: Eerdmans, 1965), 6.
22. Lewis, *The Horse and His Boy*, 116.
23. Ibid.
24. Ibid., 129–130.
25. Ibid., 127.
26. Ibid., 172, 173, 179, 180.
27. Ibid., 173.
28. Ibid., 175–176.
29. Ibid., 172.
30. Colin Manlove, *The Chronicles of Narnia: The Patterning of a Fantastic World* (Boston: Twayne, 1993), 89.
31. From an unpublished letter in the C. S. Lewis collection at the Marion E. Wade Center, Wheaton College, Illinois.

CHAPTER 5: VILLAINY MEETS VICIOUSNESS
1. C. S. Lewis, *The Lion, the Witch, and the Wardrobe: A Story for Children* (New York: Macmillan, 1950), 98.
2. Walker Percy, *Lost in the Cosmos: The Last Self-Help Book* (New York: Farrar, Straus & Giroux, 1983), 254.
3. C. S. Lewis, "On Three Ways of Writing for Children," in *On Stories, and Other Essays on Literature* (New York: Harcourt Brace Jovanovich, 1966), 31.
4. Lewis, *The Lion, the Witch, and the Wardrobe*, 14.
5. Ibid., 26.
6. Elisabeth Elliot, *Shadow of the Almighty* (New York: Harper, 1958; San Francisco: Harper and Row, 1989, first Harper and Row paperback edition), 108. Citation is to the paperback edition.
7. Lewis, *The Lion, the Witch, and the Wardrobe*, 113–114.
8. Ibid., 114.
9. Ibid.
10. Ibid.
11. Ibid., 125–126.
12. Ibid., 132–133.
13. Jeffrey D. Schultz and John G. West Jr., eds., *C. S. Lewis Readers' Encyclopedia* (Grand Rapids: Zondervan, 1998), 262.
14. C. S. Lewis, *The Magician's Nephew* (New York: Macmillan, 1955), 51.

15. Ibid., 53.
16. Ibid., 53, 55.
17. Ibid., 55.
18. C. S. Lewis, *The Great Divorce* (New York: Macmillan, 1946), 126–127.
19. Lewis, *The Magician's Nephew*, 85.
20. Ibid., 87.
21. Ibid., 89–90.
22. Ibid., 90.
23. C. S. Lewis, *The Problem of Pain* (New York: Macmillan, 1944; Macmillan Paperbacks edition,1962), 114. Citation is to the paperback edition.
24. Ibid.
25. Lewis, *The Magician's Nephew*, 16–17.
26. Ibid., 17.
27. Ibid., 161.
28. C. S. Lewis, *The Silver Chair* (New York: Macmillan, 1953), 141.
29. Ibid., 148.
30. Ibid., 150.
31. Ibid., 153–154.
32. Ibid., 131.
33. C. S. Lewis, *The Screwtape Letters and Screwtape Proposes a Toast* (New York: Macmillan, 1961), 143–144.
34. C. S. Lewis, *Prince Caspian: The Return to Narnia* (New York: Macmillan, 1952), 139–140.
35. Ibid., 140.
36. Ibid.
37. Ibid., 140–141.
38. Ibid., 142.

CHAPTER 6: VINDICATION AND VALEDICTION

1. C. S. Lewis, *The Last Battle* (New York: Macmillan, 1956), 150.
2. C. S. Lewis, *Mere Christianity* (New York: Macmillan, first paperback edition, 1960), 66.
3. Lewis, *The Last Battle*, 15–16.
4. Ibid., 25.
5. Ibid.
6. Ibid., 28.
7. Ibid., 28–29.
8. Ibid., 31.

9. Ibid.
10. Ibid., 32.
11. Ibid., 41.
12. Ibid., 69.
13. Ibid., 149.
14. Ibid., 124.
15. Ibid., 126.
16. For a discussion of the "realism of presentation," see C. S. Lewis, *An Experiment in Criticism* (Cambridge: Cambridge University Press, 1961), 57–73.
17. Lewis, *The Last Battle*, 127.
18. Ibid., 156–157.
19. Ibid., 170.
20. Ibid., 173.
21. C. S. Lewis, *The Problem of Pain* (New York: Macmillan, 1944; Macmillan Paperbacks edition, 1962), 132. Citation is to the paperback edition.

EPILOGUE

1. C. S. Lewis, *Transposition and Other Addresses* (London: G. Bles, 1949), 12.
2. C. S. Lewis, "Meditation in a Toolshed," in *God in the Dock*, ed. Walter Hooper (Grand Rapids: Eerdmans, 1970), 67–68.
3. Ibid.
4. C. S. Lewis, *The Voyage of the "Dawn Treader"* (New York: Macmillan, 1952), 175.
5. Lewis, "Meditation in a Toolshed."
6. S. Lewis, "The Empty Universe," in *God in the Dock*, ed. Walter Hooper (Grand Rapids: Eerdmans, 1970), 134–135.
7. Ibid.
8. Walker Percy, *Lost in the Cosmos: The Last Self-Help Book* (New York: Farrar, Straus & Giroux, 1983), 254.
9. Lyle W. Dorsett and Marjorie Lamp Mead, eds., *C. S. Lewis: Letters to Children* (New York: Macmillan, 1985), 45.
10. C. S. Lewis, *The Four Loves* (New York: Harcourt Brace, 1960), 188.
11. C. S. Lewis, "Sometimes Fairy Stories May Say Best What's to Be Said," in *Of Other Worlds: Essays & Stories* (New York: Harcourt, Brace, & World, 1966), 37.

12. C. S. Lewis, *Surprised by Joy: The Shape of My Early Life* (New York: Harcourt Brace & World, 1955), 21.

13. C. S. Lewis, quoted in Sheldon Vanauken, *A Severe Mercy* (San Francisco: Harper, 1987), 92–93.

14. C. S. Lewis, *The Problem of Pain* (New York: Macmillan, 1944; Macmillan Paperbacks edition, 1962), 103. Citation is to the paperback edition.

15. Blaise Pascal, *Pensées,* trans. W. F. Trotter, section IV, line 277.

16. C. S. Lewis, *The Last Battle* (New York: Macmillan, 1956), 184.